JOHN STEINBECK

Modern Critical Views

Continued at back of book

Modern Critical Views

JOHN STEINBECK

Edited and with an introduction by
Harold Bloom
Sterling Professor of the Humanities
Yale University

CHELSEA HOUSE PUBLISHERS ◊ 1987
New York ◊ New Haven ◊ Philadelphia

© 1987 by Chelsea House Publishers, a division
of Chelsea House Educational Communications, Inc.,
  95 Madison Avenue, New York, NY 10016
  345 Whitney Avenue, New Haven, CT 06511
  5068B West Chester Pike, Edgemont, PA 19028

Introduction © 1987 by Harold Bloom

Printed and bound in the United States of America

10 9 8 7 6 5 4 3 2

∞ The paper used in this publication meets the minimum
requirements of the American National Standard for Permanence
of Paper for Printed Library Materials, Z39.48-1984.

Library of Congress Cataloging-in-Publication Data

John Steinbeck.
    (Modern critical views)
    Bibliography: p.
    Includes index.
    Summary: A selection of criticism, arranged in
chronological order of publication, devoted to the
fiction of John Steinbeck.
    1. Steinbeck, John, 1902–1968—Criticism and
interpretation. [1. Steinbeck, John, 1902–1968—
Criticism and interpretation. 2. American literature—
Criticism and interpretation] I. Bloom, Harold.
II. Series.
PS3537.T3234Z7154 1987   813'.52   86–29958
ISBN 0–87754–635–5 (alk. paper)

Contents

Editor's Note

This book brings together what I judge to be the best criticism that has been published on the fiction of John Steinbeck, arranged in the chronological order of its original publication. I am grateful to Peter Childers for his aid as a researcher for this volume.

My introduction centers on *The Grapes of Wrath,* and seeks to define both its limitations and its abiding value. Donald Weeks begins the chronological sequence of criticism with a dignified lament for Steinbeck's increasingly fatal tendency towards acute sentimentalism.

Richard Astro, studying the influence of the marine biologist Edward Ricketts upon Steinbeck, finds in the movement between *Cannery Row* and *The Wayward Bus* the waning of Ricketts's vision of the cosmic unity of all life. *The Grapes of Wrath,* certainly Steinbeck's finest single achievement, is viewed by Howard Levant as a mature prose epic successful on its own terms for its first three quarters, but then yielding to flaws in its final portion. Steinbeck's naturalism is defended by Warren French, who finds however that the naturalistic stance is abandoned by Steinbeck after the Second World War.

Arthur F. Kinney, in a retrospective reading of *Tortilla Flat,* tries to defend it as the overt courting of a necessary fiction, and so less a mixture of sentimentality and burlesque than a depiction of our need for sentimentality and burlesque. The strong self-identities of Steinbeck's women in his short stories are studied by Marilyn L. Mitchell, while Jackson J. Benson focuses upon Steinbeck's own self-identifications of his role as novelist with that of scientist.

The Grapes of Wrath is analyzed by John J. Conder as an Emersonian instance of the self being both determined by nature and also transcending nature, in strong contrast to Theodore Dreiser's most characteristic attitudes. The English novelist Anthony Burgess shrewdly notes Steinbeck's anxiety of influence in regard to Hemingway and then movingly praises

Steinbeck as a writer who lived for writing. Louis Owens returns us to the dignified pathos with which Steinbeck invested *Of Mice and Men,* a pathos founded upon "the dream of man's commitment to man." In the book's final essay, a brief grace note on Abra in *East of Eden,* Mimi Reisel Gladstein finds that she is instrumental to the novel's optimistic conclusion.

Introduction

It is eighteen years since John Steinbeck died, and while his popularity as a novelist still endures, his critical reputation has suffered a considerable decline. His honors were many and varied, and included the Nobel Prize and the United States Medal of Freedom. His best novels came early in his career: *In Dubious Battle* (1936); *Of Mice and Men* (1937); *The Grapes of Wrath* (1939). Nothing after that, including *East of Eden* (1952), bears rereading. It would be good to record that rereading his three major novels is a valuable experience, from an aesthetic as well as an historical perspective.

Of Mice and Men, an economical work, really a novella, retains considerable power, marred by an intense sentimentality. But *In Dubious Battle* is now quite certainly a period piece, and is of more interest to social historians than to literary critics. *The Grapes of Wrath,* still Steinbeck's most famous and popular novel, is a very problematical work, and very difficult to judge. As story, or rather, chronicle, it lacks invention, and its characters are not persuasive representations of human inwardness. The book's wavering strength is located elsewhere, in a curious American transformation of biblical substance and style that worked splendidly in Whitman and Hemingway, but seems to work only fitfully in Steinbeck.

Steinbeck suffers from too close a comparison with Hemingway, his authentic precursor though born only three years before his follower. I think that Steinbeck's aesthetic problem *was* Hemingway, whose shadow always hovered too near. Consider the opening of *The Grapes of Wrath:*

> To the red country and part of the gray country of Oklahoma, the last rains came gently, and they did not cut the scarred earth. The plows crossed and recrossed the rivulet marks. The last rains lifted the corn quickly and scattered weed colonies and grass along the sides of the roads so that the gray country and the dark red country began to disappear under a green cover. In the last part of May the sky grew pale and the clouds

1

that had hung in high puffs for so long in the spring were dissipated. The sun flared down on the growing corn day after day until a line of brown spread along the edge of each green bayonet. The clouds appeared, and went away, and in a while they did not try any more. The weeds grew darker green to protect themselves, and they did not spread any more. The surface of the earth crusted, a thin hard crust, and as the sky became pale, so the earth became pale, pink in the red country and white in the gray country.

In the water-cut gullies the earth dusted down in dry little streams. Gophers and ant lions started small avalanches. And as the sharp sun struck day after day, the leaves of the young corn became less stiff and erect; they bent in a curve at first, and then, as the central ribs of strength grew weak, each leaf tilted downward. Then it was June, and the sun shone more fiercely. The brown lines on the corn leaves widened and moved in on the central ribs. The weeds frayed and edged back toward their roots. The air was thin and the sky more pale; and every day the earth paled.

This is not so much biblical style as mediated by Ernest Hemingway, as it is Hemingway assimilated to Steinbeck's sense of biblical style. The monosyllabic diction is hardly the mode of the King James Version, but certainly is Hemingway's. I give, very nearly at random, passages from *The Sun Also Rises:*

We passed through a town and stopped in front of the posada, and the driver took on several packages. Then we started on again, and outside the town the road commenced to mount. We were going through farming country with rocky hills that sloped down into the fields. The grain-fields went up the hillsides. Now as we went higher there was a wind blowing the grain. The road was white and dusty, and the dust rose under the wheels and hung in the air behind us. The road climbed up into the hills and left the rich grain-fields below. Now there were only patches of grain on the bare hillsides and on each side of the water-courses. We turned sharply out to the side of the road to give room to pass to a long string of six mules, following one after the other, hauling a high-hooded wagon loaded with freight. The wagon and the mules were covered with dust. Close behind was another string of mules and another wagon. This was loaded with lumber, and the arriero driving the mules leaned back and put on the thick wooden brakes as we passed. Up here the country was quite barren and the hills were rocky and hard-baked clay furrowed by the rain.

The bus climbed steadily up the road. The country was barren and rocks stuck up through the clay. There was no grass beside the road. Looking back we could see the country spread out below. Far back the fields were squares of green and brown on the hillsides. Making the horizon were the brown mountains. They were strangely shaped. As we climbed higher the horizon kept changing. As the bus ground slowly up the road we could see other mountains coming up in the south. Then the road came over the crest, flattened out, and went into a forest. It was a forest of cork oaks, and the sun came through the trees in patches, and there were cattle grazing back in the trees. We went through the forest and the road came out and turned along a rise of land, and out ahead of us was a rolling green plain, with dark mountains beyond it. These were not like the brown, heat-baked mountains we had left behind. These were wooded and there were clouds coming down from them. The green plain stretched off. It was cut by fences and the white of the road showed through the trunks of a double line of trees that crossed the plain toward the north. As we came to the edge of the rise we saw the red roofs and white houses of Burguete ahead strung out on the plain, and away off on the shoulder of the first dark mountain was the gray metal-sheathed roof of the monastery of Roncevalles.

Hemingway's Basque landscapes are described with an apparent literalness and in what seems at first a curiously dry tone, almost flat in its evident lack of significant emotion. But a closer reading suggests that the style here is itself a metaphor for a passion and a nostalgia that is both defensive and meticulous. The contrast between rich soil and barren ground, between wooded hills and heat-baked mountains, is a figure for the lost potency of Jake Barnes, but also for a larger sense of the lost possibilities of life. Steinbeck, following after Hemingway, cannot learn the lesson. He gives us a vision of the Oklahoma Dust Bowl, and it is effective enough, but it is merely a landscape where a process of entropy has been enacted. It has a social and economic meaning, but as a vision of loss lacks spiritual and personal intensity. Steinbeck is more overtly biblical than Hemingway, but too obviously so. We feel that the Bible's sense of meaning in land-scape has returned from the dead in Hemingway's own colors, but hardly in Steinbeck's.

If Steinbeck is not an original or even an adequate stylist, if he lacks skill in plot, and power in the mimesis of character, what then remains in his work, except its fairly constant popularity with an immense number of liberal middlebrows, both in his own country and abroad? Certainly, he aspired beyond his aesthetic means. If the literary Sublime, or contest for the highest place, involves persuading the reader to yield up easier plea-sures for more difficult pleasures, and it does, then Steinbeck modestly should have avoided Emerson's American Sublime, but he did not. Desir-ing it both ways, he fell into bathos in everything he wrote, even in *Of Mice and Men* and *The Grapes of Wrath*.

Yet Steinbeck had many of the legitimate impulses of the Sublime writer, and of his precursors Whitman and Hemingway in particular. Like them, he studied the nostalgias, the aboriginal sources that were never available for Americans, and like them he retained a profound hope for the American as natural man and natural woman. Unlike Whitman and Hem-ingway and the origin of this American tradition, Emerson, Steinbeck had no capacity for the nuances of literary irony. He had read Emerson's essay "The Over-Soul" as his precursors had, but Steinbeck literalized it. Emer-son, canniest where he is most the Idealist, barbs his doctrine of "that Unity, that Over-soul, within which every man's particular being is con-tained and made one with all other." In Emerson, that does not involve the sacrifice of particular being, and is hardly a program for social action:

> We live in succession, in division, in parts, in particles. Mean-time within man is the soul of the whole. . . .
> The soul knows only the soul; all else is idle weeds for her wearing.

There always have been Emersonians of the Left, like Whitman and Steinbeck, and Emersonians of the Right, like Henry James and Wallace Stevens. Emerson himself, rather gingerly planted on the moderate Left, evaded all positions. Social action is also an affair of succession, division, parts, particles; if "the soul knows only the soul," then the soul cannot know doctrines, or even human suffering. Steinbeck, socially generous, a writer on the left, structured the doctrine of *The Grapes of Wrath* on Jim Casy's literalization of Emerson's vision: "Maybe all men got one big soul and everybody's a part of it." Casy, invested by Steinbeck with a rough eloquence that would have moved Emerson, speaks his orator's epitaph just before he is martyred: "They figger I'm a leader 'cause I talk so much." He is a leader, an Okie Moses, and he dies a fitting death for the visionary of an Exodus.

I remain uneasy about my own experience of rereading *The Grapes of Wrath*. Steinbeck is not one of the inescapable American novelists of our century; he cannot be judged in close relation to Cather, Dreiser, and Faulkner, Hemingway and Fitzgerald, Nathanael West, Ralph Ellison, and Thomas Pynchon. Yet there are no canonical standards worthy of human respect that could exclude *The Grapes of Wrath* from a serious reader's esteem. Compassionate narrative that addresses itself so directly to the great social questions of its era is simply too substantial a human achievement to be dismissed. Whether a human strength, however generously worked through, is also an aesthetic value, in a literary narrative, is one of those larger issues that literary criticism scarcely knows how to decide. One might desire *The Grapes of Wrath* to be composed differently, whether as plot or as characterization, but wisdom compels one to be grateful for the novel's continued existence.

DONALD WEEKS

Steinbeck against Steinbeck

When the boys have killed the bottle and begun on the second gallon of dago red, then men are good, and what they mean to do has been done. Intention becomes fact. There is no tomorrow, no today. There is yesterday always. Then some voice is predestined to sing, "What's the matter with——? He's all right!" Well—what's the matter with Steinbeck? To listen to the professional critics, "He's all right!" To listen to the critics: they said of *Cannery Row,* "another of his small miracles," "his most satisfactory manner," "so boundless an enthusiasm for human nature," "the warm humanity"; they said of *The Wayward Bus,* "very much a *must* novel," "a warm flow of vitality," "his emphasis on healthy positive values." They call Steinbeck "the writer with the most evident love for his fellow humans"; they find in him "the greatest feeling for the basic human values."

Theirs are the louder voices, and what they seem to be saying is that *Cannery Row* and *The Wayward Bus* are as good as *Tortilla Flat* and *In Dubious Battle.* Or, if they are not so good as the earlier books, they are not comparable and are good of their kind. Theirs are the louder voices, but the sharper critics have insisted on the basic sentimentalism in Steinbeck, and, on the other side of that sentimentalism, on the cruelty it covers up. The answer has been to admit Steinbeck's sentimentalism. Yes, Steinbeck is sentimental; he has called himself sentimental.

There is this to be said for sentimentality: that to affairs of no consequence it gives consequence. It must never be serious; it must never

From *The Pacific Spectator* 1, no. 4 (Autumn 1947). © 1947 by The Pacific Coast Committee for the Humanities of the American Council of Learned Societies.

be maudlin; it may be vinous, like the forty Scandinavians with glasses in
their hands who solemnly sang,

> Sent Looisss Voomans, vit you diment errings
> Chessed det men aroun de apon strings.

Steinbeck said, "It was unique in international feelings. It was very beautiful." Always, with Steinbeck, the reader is first puzzled by the tone of such
remarks: serious or not? Because Steinbeck rationalizes his sentimentality.

In *Tortilla Flat,* Steinbeck wrote a masterpiece of sentimentality. In the
foreword to the Modern Library Edition (the book appeared first in 1935,
the Modern Library reprint of it in 1937) he was unwilling to let the story
stand for what it was. He described the citizens of *Tortilla Flat* as "people
whom I know and like, people who merge successfully with their habitat.
In men this is called philosophy, and it is a fine thing." He protested that
he would never have written about these people if he had known that they
would be thought quaint by "literary slummers." Steinbeck then described
the elder sister of a school friend and said "still I can't think of the
hoor-lady as (that nastiest of words) a prostitute, nor of the *piojo's* many
uncles, those jolly men who sometimes gave us nickels, as her clients." The
foreword to *Tortilla Flat* ends with a protest that *Cannery Row* denies,
"But I shall never again subject to the vulgar touch of the *decent* these
good people of laughter and kindness, of honest lusts and direct eyes, of
courtesy beyond politeness. It will not happen again." I can't see much
difference between this foreword and denying that grandmother is a drunk-
ard because she's so nice to the kids.

To me, the foreword is a rationalization in terms of the philosophy
which from 1935 on Steinbeck fails to bring into coherence with his art.
To me, it is a philosophy which encourages Steinbeck to rationalize his
sentimentality. This philosophy he may have acquired from his friend, Dr.
Edward Ricketts, without ever understanding its relation to his art, and
especially to his sentimentality. It is a philosophy best expressed in *Sea of
Cortez* (1941), written in collaboration with Dr. Ricketts, and worst
expressed in *Cannery Row* (1945), where Ricketts appears slightly disguised
as Doc, and where passages of *Sea of Cortez* reappear as fiction. *Cannery
Row* is dedicated to "Ed Ricketts who knows why or should." Steinbeck
came to know Ricketts when the Steinbecks moved to Pacific Grove in
1930. Edward Ricketts runs a marine biological supply house in Monterey. He is the author of *Between Pacific Tides* and of the annotated
bibliography which makes up half of *Sea of Cortez.* It is said that Steinbeck financed the expedition to Lower California described in *Sea of*

Cortez, A Leisurely Journal of Travel and Research. There is no statement of the division of labor in the book. The writing is, of course, John Steinbeck's. It is fair to assume that the ideas of the narrative are shared by both authors. To me, the confusions in the book, whether the speculations are playful (as Steinbeck called them) or not, are real.

I want to quote two long passages from *Sea of Cortez* and then have done with that kind of quoting, which is no substitute for reading the book. Much of *Sea of Cortez* is an essay in favor of nonteleological thinking, and much of it is an essay on the life of our times critical in a way more in the spirit of Jeremiah than of the scientist who accepts the fact that "*a thing is because it is.*" The italics are not mine.

> What we personally conceive by the term "teleological think-ing," as exemplified by the notion about the shiftless unem-ployed, is most frequently associated with the evaluating of causes and effects, the purposiveness of events. This kind of thinking considers changes and cures—what "should be"—in the terms of an end pattern (which is often a subjective or an anthropomorphic projection); it presumes the bettering of con-ditions, often, unfortunately, without achieving more than a most superficial understanding of those conditions. In their sometimes intolerant refusal to face facts as they are, teleologi-cal notions may substitute a fierce but ineffectual attempt to change conditions which are assumed to be undesirable, in place of the understanding acceptance which would pave the way for a more sensible attempt at any change which might still be indicated.
>
> Non-teleological ideas derive through "is" thinking, associ-ated with natural selection, as Darwin seems to have under-stood it. They imply depth, fundamentalism, and clarity—seeing beyond traditional or personal projections. They consider events as outgrowths and expressions rather than as results; conscious acceptance as a desideratum, and certainly as an all-important prerequisite. Nonteleological thinking concerns itself primarily not with what should be, or could be, or might be, but rather with what actually "is"—attempting at most to answer the already sufficiently difficult questions *what or how,* instead of *why.*

It would be easy to make fun of the language of this passage. What-ever one is arguing for is always clear, deep, and fundamental. There is no point in discussing the relative merits of teleological and nonteleological thinking. Obviously, after centuries of one kind of thinking, another kind has full rights to explore the universe for whatever it can get out of it. But from their nonteleological thinking, Steinbeck and Ricketts draw an attitude toward "the incompetent or maladjusted or unlucky" that is relevant to Steinbeck's fiction. The fact that the unemployed are made up of the incompetent involves no causality.

> Collectively it's just "so"; collectively, it's related to the fact that animals produce more offspring than the world can support. The units may be blamed as individuals, but as members of society they cannot be blamed. Any given individual very possibly may transfer from the underprivileged into the more fortunate group by better luck or by improved aggressiveness or competence, but all cannot be so benefited whatever their strivings, and the large population will be unaffected. The seventy-thirty ratio will remain, with merely a reassortment of the units. And no blame, at least no social fault, imputes to these people; they are what they are "because" natural conditions are what they are. And so far as we selfishly are concerned we can rejoice that they, rather than we, represent the low extreme, since they must be one.
>
> So if one is very aggressive he will be able to obtain work even under the most sub-normal economic conditions, but only because there are others, less aggressive than he, who serve in his stead as potential government wards. In the same way, the sight of a half-wit should never depress us, since his extreme and the extreme of his kind, so affects the mean standard that we, hatless, coatless, often bewhiskered, thereby will be regarded as only a little odd. And similarly, we cannot justly approve the success manuals that tell our high-school graduates how to get a job—there being jobs for only half of them!
>
> This type of thinking unfortunately annoys many people. It may especially arouse the anger of women, who regard it as cold, even brutal, although actually it would be tender and understanding, certainly more real and less illusionary and even less blaming, than the more conventional methods of consideration. And the value of it as a tool in increased understanding cannot be denied.

There is much more like this in *Sea of Cortez* on the adjustment of primitive peoples to their environment, on man as a product of disease, on the virtues of laziness and of alcohol, on the tremendous wastefulness of life. These speculations, as they are called in the index of *Sea of Cortez,* playful speculations if we take Steinbeck at his word, could be accepted as playful if they did not turn up in *Cannery Row* with such disastrous effect.

My biologist friends tell me that speculations on purpose have ruined many a biologist, who if he were a good biologist would be willing to leave teleology to the philosopher, who if he were a good philosopher would leave it to the psychologist. For the artist, his philosophy may be the sum of the books he has read and the friends he has listened to. I like playfully to speculate what the reading of W. H. Sheldon's *Varieties of Human Physique* and *Varieties of Temperament* would have taught Stein-beck and Ricketts and how Sheldon would explain the glorification of the viscerotonic boys (those who live by the stomach) of *Tortilla Flat* by the possibly cerebrotonic Steinbeck. I am sure that Steinbeck would underline Sheldon's statement that "it may be well, in the long run, that we cannot get at viscerotonia, for this component may constitute a kind of insurance or reservoir of safety for the species."

It is just at this point that the trouble starts. The philosophy of *Sea of Cortez* commits Steinbeck to realism, and Steinbeck is not a realist. He cannot describe objectively. His feelings commit him to celebration. When you come right down to it, forty Scandinavians with glasses in their hands singing "St. Louis Blues" contribute about as much to international under-standing as Marlene Dietrich did to the invasion of Africa when she kicked off her shoes and in her bare feet followed her man across the burning sands of the Sahara (have you forgotten the scene in *Morocco?*). The forty Scandinavians are "unique" and "beautiful"—and of no consequence if we are to take them seriously as we are asked to take seriously Mack and the boys in *Cannery Row.*

From the idea that a "thing is because it is," a writer can derive a wide range of emotions. One of these emotions, perhaps the narrowest and most intense but also the most transforming, is the sentimentality which takes the incompetent, the maladjusted, the unlucky Mack and the boys and describes them as "the Virtues, the Graces, the Beauties" of modern Monterey, where other men are destroying themselves in competition. Steinbeck prays for the boys, "Our Father who art in nature, who has given the gift of survival to the coyote, the common brown rat, the English sparrow, the house fly and the moth, must have a great and overwhelming love for no-goods and blots-on-the-town and bums, Mack and the boys. Virtues and graces and laziness and zest. Our Father who art in nature."

Such language is not descriptive of things as they are. It is a language that gives value to certain things because they survive, as more of us survive than Steinbeck is willing to admit. Since the sentimentalist likes to believe that men are good by instinct—with Steinbeck the instinct to survive *is* that good—he has trouble with choice. At least men think they choose. Steinbeck says that Mack and the boys avoid the traps of our culture, "walk around the poison, step over the noose." The question seems to be whether the traps and nooses which Steinbeck finds in modern life are what he says they are.

Sea of Cortez contrasts the neuroticism of modern culture with what Steinbeck feels is the naturalness of primitive men, such as the Indians of Lower California. Without exaggerating the perfections of primitive life, Steinbeck yet makes it clear that modern man has lost some kind of health which primitive man has. He is made angry by the great gap between our ideals and our practice. "And . . . in our structure of society, the so-called and considered good qualities are invariable concomitants of failure, while the bad ones are the cornerstones of success." It is a long passage in *Sea of Cortez,* and Doc says the same thing in almost the same words in *Cannery Row:*

> It has always seemed strange to me. . . . The things we admire in men, kindness and generosity, openness, honesty, understanding and feeling, are the concomitants of failure in our system. And those traits we detest, sharpness, greed, acquisitiveness, meanness, egotism, and self-interest, are the traits of success. And while men admire the quality of the first they love the produce of the second.

Doc likes Mack and the boys because they "are healthy and curiously clean. They can do what they want. They can satisfy their appetites without calling them something else." In *Sea of Cortez,* Steinbeck (and Ricketts) writes, "In an animal other than man we would replace the term 'good' with 'weak survival quotient' and the term 'bad' with 'strong survival quotient.'" Doc thinks that Mack and the boys "survive in this particular world better than other people." That's bad? Or good? As Sheldon says, "The life of a viscerotonic individual seems to be organized primarily to serve the gut." That's Mack and the boys.

To be fair, Steinbeck does qualify, but only once so far as I can find. In *Cannery Row:*

> It's all fine to say, "Time will heal everything, this too shall pass away. People will forget"—and things like that when you

are not involved, but when you are, there is no passage of time, people do not forget, and you are in the middle of something that does not change. Doc didn't know the pain and self-destructive criticism in the Palace Flophouse or he might have tried to do something about it.

But Doc is too like the boys: "you know how they tried to give me a party. That was their impulse."

At this point I'll take the risk of being misunderstood. I want to call the celebration of impulse in Steinbeck the philosophy of the wino. I am not, of course, applying the term to Steinbeck himself. But any writer can get just as tight with a typewriter as with alcohol. Sentimentality is the worst jag a writer can get. When Steinbeck gets sentimental, life becomes warm, beautiful, satisfying, and when that happens, I can't see how Steinbeck differs from the boys at work on the second gallon. Then men explain all, rationalize everything, and cannot leave alone the reasons for their own failure. Then writers write about flies "very happy" eating cake; about the smell of grass and lupine so sweet it sets you "panting almost sexually"; and about hills—"rounded, woman-like hills, soft and sexual as flesh," an image I thought Somerset Maugham had "done in" with the hills of Nebraska in "Rain." I take the three illustrations from *The Wayward Bus*.

The sentimentalist puts himself in the position of limiting his range of expression to absolutes. For contrast, Steinbeck turns to cruelty and dirt. No one can say that men are not cruel and dirty minded. They are, and often gratuitously. But a writer who relies on an alternation of black and white makes of his novel a primitive movie in which the frames move so slowly that the eye catches the flicker. *Cannery Row* and *The Wayward Bus* are in British slang "flicks." The blacks and the whites never merge.

The Josh Billings story, chapter 12 of *Cannery Row,* is an example. It's a vulgar, funny story. It's the kind of story the boys in the frat house tell the pledges at dinner. Since one of the pledges will remain an adolescent for the next forty years, it's the kind of story you may hear at some dinner table. Chapter 12 comes in the middle of the trip the boys take to the Carmel Valley frog hunting. The death of Josh Billings in 1885 has nothing to do with the frog hunt. *Cannery Row* being no *Tristram Shandy*, no monumental book filled with long, wonderful irrelevancies, so strong a fragment calls attention to the slightness of the book, which is not husky enough to sustain the incident. The story serves as some subconscious check on Steinbeck's sentimentalism toward Gay and the Model T. Gay has

just been described in chapter 11 as "the little mechanic of God, the St.
Francis of all things that turn and twist and explode, the St. Francis of
coils and armatures and gears." And John Steinbeck knows what Gay
would say to that.

In *The Wayward Bus,* an example of cruel funny business (to quote
the blurb, "all of them invented by Steinbeck") is the rape of Mrs.
Pritchard by Mr. Pritchard. Since Mrs. Pritchard has learned a lesson from
the girls on the bus, she bites her lip, scratches her cheeks till they bleed,
and rubs dirt in. The purpose of these wounds is to get an orchid house.
There is a moral ambiguity to this episode that is curious, but more
pertinent to this criticism is the inadequacy of the scene as art. Such a
scene leaves me cold. In *The Wayward Bus,* I am too aware of Steinbeck's
trying to claim humanity for his characters by a conscious use of psychology. As Mildred Pritchard said to Juan Chicoy, "I know thousands of case
histories." And this one sounds straight out of Krafft-Ebing, a book I
thought a fellow got out of his system in college. The characters of much
modern fiction are flat because writers bring to characterization their
reading of psychology, and that knowledge runs to types as transparent as
the cast of *Orphan Annie.* In *Of Mice and Men* and *The Moon Is Down,*
Steinbeck tried "an experiment in making a play that can be read or a
novel that can be played . . . to find a new form that will take some of the
techniques of both." As Lewis Gannett says in his introduction to *The
Portable Steinbeck,* "This was a problem that was to concern him for
years." *The Wayward Bus* reads like a movie, an uncensored movie. Any
writer finds a form which allows the fullest expression of what he does
best, but the different ways in which we read a novel and see a play are
worth remembering. The reader asks more of a novel in characterization.
He does not want men and women simplified for him. He wants them
whole.

The novel of types is a form that carries great authority when the
types are used for satire, and when one type—say, the sentimental—is used
to show a likeness to another type—the cruel. But when the cruel is used
to compensate for the sentimental, I am reminded of Dickens's saying (and
who should know better?) that any bungler can stir the emotions. Tears and
goose flesh are the very surface of emotion.

What *is* the matter with Steinbeck? I repeat the question because I
cannot take seriously *Cannery Row, The Wayward Bus,* or *The Moon Is
Down,* which I think is even more limited by its occasional character as a
novel of the war. It is by his fiction that Steinbeck will be judged. There is
no novel since *The Grapes of Wrath* (1939) to justify a statement that he is

still developing as a writer. To go back and quote Mildred Pritchard in full, "I know thousands of case histories, but I can't make the advances."

Of one thing I am sure: there is no simple answer to the question. Each one of us would resent a simplification of personal problems that we find complex. In the artist the complexity of a problem is increased by the radar-like sensibility of the man who is usually conscious of what is happening to him and is made uneasy by any rationalization to which he turns. I see no reason not to say certain things about Steinbeck with the understanding that they are parts of a whole beyond any critic's knowledge. Steinbeck wrote of *Sea of Cortez*, "The rage and contempt of the critics will be amusing and like old times." I am not writing in rage or contempt but out of a sincere concern that Steinbeck's later novels have been so inhuman, so deeply contemptuous, I would say, of men and women, for I call that art contemptuous which asks me to take its black and white as the color of life.

Steinbeck has spoken his fear of success, as an artist should, but success has brought him wealth and that mobility of the rich which often makes them come back home as mere visitors and tourists. The tempering of poverty that Steinbeck knew in his earlier years is not necessarily a lifetime discipline. To be able to come and go as he likes may be of no advantage to a writer whose best work is drawn from a single source: California. For one kind of artist the legend of Antaeus, who lost his strength when he lost his touch with earth, may be more than legend, may be the very necessary warning of the limits of his art. In choosing scenes that he already knew for *Cannery Row* and *The Wayward Bus*, Steinbeck seems to be acknowledging this limitation of his art, but in a superficial way.

It is obvious that for the successful writer in America there is some failure of criticism to do its job. I doubt that Steinbeck's publishers or agents or friends say very much that matters about the quality of his later works. These are the people who count as critics, because an author can easily shake off the reviews. I should say the evidence is clear that there is now no critic intimate with Steinbeck, no one to challenge the writer's best. A critic comparing Steinbeck with Dickens (on the basis of their sentimentality and love of men) does a disservice to Steinbeck because there is nothing to show that Steinbeck is one of the great physical phenomena of writing like Dickens, Balzac, or Thomas Wolfe. His best work indicates that he is not a naïve artist, but profits by care.

Steinbeck is said to fear being thought arty. We all know what he means. But the people he celebrates, at least in *Cannery Row,* are not

much different from the "artists" he fears. The world of the incompetent,
the maladjusted, and the unlucky usually overlaps that of the poor artist.
The difference between Mack and the boys and the artist is that the artist gets
something done. If he doesn't, he is one of the boys. A real artist can be
one of the boys just so far and no further. He can share with them all
freedom from responsibilities except the responsibility to his own compe-
tence. I had hoped to finish without mentioning the confusion of our
times, but I am not going to be able to. In a more conventional society,
Steinbeck might well have been arty, but being confused like the rest of us
as to where he belongs, he has turned to identify himself with the group
traditionally closest to the Bohemian. He has identified himself with the
world of good intentions.

The best intentions of Steinbeck's characters find easy, natural, and
sometimes their only fulfillment in sex. I want to conclude, then, by saying
something about Steinbeck's attitude toward sex. Here I find him so
surprisingly naïve in his assumptions that by contrast the *Ladies Home
Journal* or the *Reader's Digest* are distilled sophistication on the same
subject. Steinbeck plainly assumes that the people he describes have the
secret of sexual success. He seems to take it for granted that primitive
peoples have no sexual problems. I wonder how far he has been influenced
by D. H. Lawrence, whom he was said to admire. I could take the sex in
Steinbeck if it were not for two uses he makes of it. One is its use to create
suspense. Steinbeck seems not to understand the weakness of sex as an
artistic device. With his attitude toward it, it doesn't matter who sleeps
with whom. In *The Wayward Bus*, tedium sets in early because of this fact,
which was supposed to provide the excitement of the last pages of the
novel. The other use he makes of sex is as a means to criticize middle-class
morality in America. Here he is fighting a battle already won and endan-
gering the victory by confusing the issue. The fight was not fought to
guarantee promiscuity. Man's nature takes care of that. The fight was not
fought just for freedom of expression. Some of the living men and women
who fought that fight in this country have said that they fought for
freedom to learn. This may sound like a schoolteacher talking. It's a point
on which a schoolteacher can talk if he gets around at all among kids in
college. A teacher does not simplify problems either intellectually or emotionally. He knows the practices that come naturally and the learning that
is hard won. When he doesn't know, he turns to those who are trying to
find out. I want to quote Sheldon once more. The italics are his. "A rich
background of sexual experience appears to exert about the same effect [as
psychoanalysis in enriching consciousness and bringing tolerance and

perspective], *in those who can assimilate it.* But the latter seem to be in the minority. Both psychoanalysis and overt sexuality are seen sometimes to coarsen the ordinary person, to render him more obnoxiously and more crassly sophisticated."

I thought of Steinbeck as I read in the papers of the Fourth of July weekend riot in Hollister, California. If you missed the story, this is what happened: Four thousand motorcyclists gathered in Hollister, a town of about four thousand, for a three-day meeting. The party got rough, rough enough that the sheriff had to establish a kind of martial law to put an end to the breaking of bottles in the street, the racing through the town, the driving of motorcycles into bars, the usual antics that turn a fiesta into a bust. There were all the elements of a Steinbeck novel: A country which Steinbeck knows well. The kind of men Steinbeck writes well about. The grand kermess. There was the man whose foot was cut off. There was the fellow whose friends picked the lock of the jail; he came back because he was hungry. There was the sheriff who philosophized, "You can't drink winter whiskey on a summer stomach." There were the sleepers in the haystacks. It fell together in my mind in terms of the Steinbeck who wrote *In Dubious Battle* and *The Red Pony.* It was not a novel many men could write. They know neither the country nor the people, and knowledge of them alone could spark life into the story. But when I thought of the story in terms of *Cannery Row* and *The Wayward Bus,* it didn't seem such a good idea. I thought I knew what was the matter with Steinbeck.

I could be wrong.

I want to be wrong.

RICHARD ASTRO

Intimations of a Wasteland

Despite Steinbeck's early enthusiastic support of the American war effort, there is little question but that the novelist's faith in the human species was sorely tested by his experiences in the European theater. The writer who in 1939 had posited an idealistic theory of agrarian reform as a solution to the economic and political crises in American agriculture was shaken by the irreconcilable fact that hoes and spades had yielded to howitzers and submachine guns. And despite the conviction with which he asserted his belief in the ultimate victory of free men over the herd (*The Moon Is Down*) and with which he reported seeing evidence of man's finest qualities among American soldiers in the most hellish of wartime situations (*Once There Was a War*), by 1944, Steinbeck's interest in and sympathy for the war had worn thin.

In February 1943, the novelist told Webster Street that Ricketts had developed a philosophical pattern of thinking that enabled him to accept the war and write about it without liking it. But for a goal-oriented novelist like Steinbeck, nonteleological philosophical patterns of understanding-acceptance were impossible. Moreover, the war had taken a heavy toll on John Steinbeck the novelist. *Bombs Away*, the communiques in *Once There Was a War,* and even *The Moon Is Down* were among his least consequential works to date, and Steinbeck knew it. And so, by 1944, Steinbeck realized that if he was going to reassert himself as a writer of good fiction, he would have to return to the subjects and locales he knew best and had written about most successfully. If Steinbeck's unusually

From *John Steinbeck and Edward F. Ricketts: The Shaping of a Novelist.* © 1973 by the University of Minnesota. University of Minnesota Press, 1973.

heavy dependence upon Ricketts's thinking which overwhelmed the fictional pattern of reality in *The Moon Is Down* drove the novelist away from any sort of literary involvement with Ricketts's ideas, the artistic inconsequence of his later war writings temporarily sent him scurrying back. Writing to Street in July 1944, Steinbeck discusses his work on a "fun book" that never mentions the war, and he indicates that while he had written many words during the past three years, for the first time in that period he was really working.

The result of this "return to work" was *Cannery Row* (1945), a novel Steinbeck described as "a mixed-up book" with a "pretty general ribbing in it." Ostensibly, the theme of *Cannery Row,* which Orville Prescott called "a sentimental glorification of weakness of mind and degeneration of character," is as foreign to Steinbeck's great political novels as those works are to *Bombs Away* and *Once There Was a War.* But a deeper, more penetrating look at the novel reveals that *Cannery Row* contains Steinbeck's greatest statement of affection for Ed Ricketts as well as the novelist's objective portrayal of the inherent shortcomings of the marine biologist's complex philosophy of life. Steinbeck returns in *Cannery Row* to his most fundamental social and philosophical concerns. It is a book about a real if unusual world and about a wonderful man at the center of that world. But, despite his love for this world and the people who inhabit it, Steinbeck orders his novel to show beyond all doubt that it is as doomed to eventual extinction as the world of Colonel Lanser's overly integrated soldiers in *The Moon Is Down.*

In many ways, *Cannery Row* is a fictional sequel to the *Log* section of *Sea of Cortez* in that Steinbeck applies directly to a work of fiction many of the philosophical premises he and Ricketts developed in the Gulf of California. Most importantly, Doc, the main character of *Cannery Row,* is the most lifelike fictional version of Ed Ricketts in the entire catalogue of Steinbeck's fiction. And even Steinbeck's statement about the manner in which he ordered the fictional pattern of reality in *Cannery Row* resembles the methods he and Ricketts used to collect faunal specimens in the Gulf:

> How can the poem and the stink and the grating noise—the quality of light, the tone, the habit and the dream—be set down alive? When you collect marine animals there are certain flat worms so delicate that they are almost impossible to capture whole, for they break and tatter under the touch. You must let them ooze and crawl of their own will onto a knife blade and then lift them gently into your bottle of sea water. And perhaps

that might be the way to write this book—to open the page and
to let the stories crawl in by themselves.

(Introduction)

In his discussion of *Cannery Row,* Joseph Fontenrose concludes that
the main issue in the novel is the way in which Steinbeck suggests that man
may "savor the hot taste of life." It will be remembered, of course, that
"the hot taste of life" was also a central concern in the *Log* where, at the
end of the trip, the authors remark that their voyage had "dimension and
tone." It was "no service to science," but "we simply liked it. We liked it
very much. The brown Indians and the gardens of the sea, and the beer
and the work, they were all one thing and we were that one thing too."

It is important to recognize, however, that the pursuit of "the hot
taste of life" in *Cannery Row* is Doc's, not necessarily Steinbeck's. For
while the author was deprived by definition of a fictional persona in the
Log, in *Cannery Row* not only could he portray Ricketts's quest for
dimension and tone, but at the same time he was able to examine the
inherent pitfalls which betray the seeker. In "About Ed Ricketts," Steinbeck recalls that he took the typescript of *Cannery Row* to Ricketts for
approval. And he notes that the marine biologist "read it through carefully, smiling, and when he had finished he said, 'Let it go that way. It is
written in kindness.' " Steinbeck surely wrote *Cannery Row* in kindness.
And yet beneath the novelist's moving account of Doc and his friends is his
penetrating look at the liabilities of a life-style which, because it denies
many of the hard facts of existence, is ultimately untenable.

In many ways, Doc is the most loved and gingerly treated character in
any Steinbeck novel. A man of broad vision, Doc owns and operates the
Western Biological Laboratory on Cannery Row and is the universal man:
"his mind had no horizon—and his sympathy had no warp." "He lived in
a world of wonders, of excitement. He was concupiscent as a rabbit and
gentle as hell."

Like Ricketts, Doc is a dedicated and accomplished marine biologist
who studies the "good, kind, sane little animals" in the Great Tide Pool
with a unique understanding of the interrelated patterns of animal life.
And no wonder, for the Great Tide Pool "is a fabulous place."

> When the tide is in, a wave-churned basin, creamy with foam,
> whipped by the combers that roll in from the whistling buoy on
> the reef. But when the tide goes out the little water world
> becomes quiet and lovely. The sea is very clear and the bottom
> becomes fantastic with hurrying, fighting, feeding, breeding

animals. Crabs rush from frond to frond of the waving algae. Starfish squat over mussels and limpets, attach their million little suckers and then slowly lift with incredible power until the prey is broken from the rock.

Doc spends much of his time in the tide pools, where the "smells of life and richness, of death and digestion, and decay and birth, burden the air." Indeed, for Doc, the tide pools are microcosmic emblems of the delicately maintained ecological balance in the holistic order of things where all life forms struggle in the unending fight for survival. Moreover, Doc knows the faunal patterns of the California coast as well as any man.

> The sea rocks and the beaches were his stockpile. He knew where everything was when he wanted it. All the articles of his trade were filed away on the coast, sea cradles here, octopi here, tube worms in another place, sea pansies in another. He knew where to get them but he could not go for them exactly when he wanted. For Nature locked up the items and only released them occasionally. Doc had to know not only the tides but when a particular low tide was good in a particular place.

Doc's laboratory is a veritable extension of the tide pool. As a supplier of marine specimens, Doc sells "the lovely animals of the sea, the sponges, tunicates, anemones, the stars and buttlestars, and sun stars, the bivalves, barnacles, the worms and shells, the fabulous and multi-form little brothers, the little moving flowers of the sea, nudibranchs and tetrabranchs." His kindness extends to every form of animal life, so that though his profession demands that on occasion he kill specimens for research, he kills only out of necessity, since "he could not even hurt a feeling for pleasure."

Doc is not only a highly competent marine biologist with a fundamental understanding of relational patterns in the "Great Organism of Life." He is also the "fountain of philosophy and science and art" on the Row. In addition to the many aquaria in his laboratory which hold an infinite variety of sea creatures, there is "a great phonograph" with hundreds of records lined up beside it, ranging from Benny Goodman to the Brandenburg Concertos. And on the walls are pinned reproductions of Daumiers, Titians, Picassos, Dalis, and Grahams (presumably Ellwood Graham).

Doc is "a lonely and set-apart man" (a quality Steinbeck detected in Ricketts as well), but at the same time he is the chief advisor to Mack and the boys, those "no-goods" and "blots-on-the-town" who are among the most enjoyable characters in any Steinbeck novel. "Mack and the boys," says Steinbeck, "are the Virtues, and Graces, the Beauties of the hurried mangled craziness of Monterey"; beloved children of "Our Father who art in Nature" who "dine delicately with the tigers, fondle the frantic heifers, and wrap up the crumbs to feed the sea gulls of Cannery Row." Doc calls Mack and the boys "your true philosophers," and he sounds much like Ricketts discussing the ill effects of material gain to the psyche when he insists that:

> In a time when people tear themselves to pieces with ambition and nervousness and covetousness, they are relaxed. All of our so-called successful men are sick men, with bad stomachs, and bad souls, but Mack and the boys are healthy and curiously clean. They can do what they want. They can satisfy their appetites without calling them something else.

Like the gentle if indolent Indians of Baja California whose laziness Ricketts believed was the proper state of mind for a contemplation of oneself in relation to the world, Mack and the boys "know everything that has ever happened in the world and possibly everything that will happen." When Doc suggests that "they will survive in this particular world better than other people," he reiterates Ricketts's faith in the survival quotient of simple people who, though poor and hungry and plagued by toothaches, do not kill themselves over things which do not concern them and so live longer and richer lives than their more prosperous neighbors who are enslaved by the products of their own technology.

"Everywhere in the world there are Mack and the boys," suggests Doc; the "sale of souls to gain the whole world is completely voluntary and almost unanimous—but not quite. . . . I've seen them in an ice-cream seller in Mexico and in an Aleut in Alaska." Here again, Steinbeck is faithful to his model, since in his "Thesis and Materials for a Script on Mexico," Ricketts discusses in detail his experiences with a sidewalk ice-cream seller in Puebla who gave his wares to customers who had no money, never doubting that they would return to pay if ever they had the money. Ricketts states that if the ice-cream seller tried to conduct business with Americans along these lines, he "would have to adopt a C.O.D. policy . . . or else he'd have to retire bankrupt from his business, with an attitude of cynicism toward the 'honest' nordamericanos to boot."

The spirit of goodwill shared by the leading denizens of Cannery Row pervades the entire novel. But the Row's unique flower of friendship reaches its apex during the famous party in Doc's laboratory which [Peter

Lisca calls] one of the "most riotous parties in American literature." And on the morning after the affair, Doc, who is still immersed in the mood of the previous evening, reads aloud from the Sanskrit poem, "Black Marigolds," as he intuitively breaks through to a realization that he has savored "the hot taste of life."

> Even now
> I know that I have savored the hot taste of life
> Lifting green cups and gold at the great feast.
> Just for a small and a forgotten time
> I have had full in my eyes from off my girl
> The whitest pouring of eternal light—

Ostensibly then, Steinbeck says in *Cannery Row* that man can savor "the hot taste of life" if he pursues a free and uninhibited existence. But there is some question whether Steinbeck regards this approach to life as a tenable solution to man's quest for meaning in an increasingly rapacious world. For while Cannery Row is a self-contained island populated by "saints and angels and martyrs and holy men," the type of behavior practiced by the Row's denizens would be inadmissable anywhere else in the world. And whenever any of the characters ventures beyond the Row's sheltered confines, he encounters suspicion and resentment.

In one instance, Steinbeck draws upon an actual event in Ricketts's life and writes that when Doc was a student at the University of Chicago he decided to take a walking trip through the southeastern United States. Doc found that the people he met could not understand why he wanted to roam about the woods like a vagabond. And although Doc "tried to explain. He said he was nervous and besides he wanted to see the country, smell the ground and look at grass and birds and trees, to savor the country, and there was no other way to do it save on foot," the people were unable to share his enthusiasm, and they disliked him.

> They scowled or shook and tapped their heads, they laughed as if they knew it was a lie and they appreciated a liar. And some, afraid for their daughters or their pigs, told him to move on, to get going, just not to stop near their place if he knew what was good for him.

Later in the novel, when Doc travels down the California coast on a collecting expedition, he is beset by an unlikely assortment of perverse hitchhikers, rude waitresses, and bounty hunters. Similarly, Mack and the boys have had distressing experiences outside the Row. Mack came to the

Row in a state of utter dejection, since everything he had ever done before had gone wrong. He tells Doc that he sought out the uninhibited, clowning life of the Row in order to flee the "serious world" which destroys clowns: " 'Same thing ever' place 'til I just got to clowning. I don't do nothin' but clown no more. Try to make the boys laugh.' "

It might be argued that Steinbeck's apparent approval of the indolent life-styles of Mack and the boys is evidence that in *Cannery Row* he "steps stage-front to proselytize his readers" about the virtues of escape. Certainly, Steinbeck enjoyed contemplating the retreats of the scientist and the loafer. But his vision of America was not so naïve as to blind him to the inevitable transciency of those life-styles. When Malcolm Cowley observed that the novel might be a "poisoned cream puff" thrown at "respectable society," Steinbeck replied that if Cowley read *Cannery Row* again, "he would see how very poisoned it was." Indeed, Steinbeck indicts what we call the "civilized world," and he correspondingly applauds life on the Row. But he reveals paradoxically (and this is the novel's real venom) that although Doc is a fountain of science, art, and philosophy, and although Mack and the boys are "the Virtues, the Graces, and the Beauties," they live insular lives and are themselves surrounded on all sides by an ever-expanding commercial society which will one day make those life-styles untenable. The party is over—"the hot taste of life" has been savored—and there is nothing left but nostalgia. *Cannery Row* ends with Doc wiping "his eyes with the back of his hand. . . . And behind the glass the rattlesnakes lay still and stared into space with their dusty frowning eyes."

Fontenrose has identified parallels between the characters of *Cannery Row* and those of *In Dubious Battle*. "Mack of *Cannery Row* looks like a deliberate burlesque of Mac in *In Dubious Battle*," and "each Mac[k] stands in complementary relation to Doc; each is a man of devices, and Doc is the objective non-teleological observer." "The Party is definitely rejected and we are invited to a party," notes Fontenrose, since Steinbeck believes that "our sad, lonely condition can be alleviated only by moments of great joy, parties, and love affairs, when we savor 'the hot taste of life.' " Because of its transient nature, however, the party is not much better than the Party. Moreover, both Docs are lonely, set-apart men, who, while able to break through to momentary insights of great misunderstanding, are in the end sustained only by their melancholy. And even apart from Steinbeck's social convictions about the weak survival quotient of the nonteleological visionary amid the chaos of the modern world, this is essentially how the novelist saw Ricketts: as a searching but troubled man, walled off a little who tried but never for more than an instant succeeded in "crashing through into the light." On the basis of Ricketts's world-view as expressed in his own writings, one might argue that Steinbeck's portrait is inaccurate and unfair. But while this argument is valid, it simply is not relevant to a study of Steinbeck's fiction. For this is the way Steinbeck saw his closest friend, and this is the way he portrayed him in *In Dubious Battle* and again in *Cannery Row*.

But while Steinbeck's portrait of his Ricketts-figure in *Cannery Row* closely resembles his treatment of Doc Burton in *In Dubious Battle,* there is a marked difference between the forces with which each must contend. Burton is defeated by the iron teleologies of the partisan Party leaders who confuse ends and means and refuse to take the time to listen to Doc's high-falutin ideas. Doc in *Cannery Row,* however, is plagued by materialistic Americans who are blind to the ecological truths of nature and to the organismic structure of life, but who, because of their unremitting possessiveness and sheer numbers, may ultimately inherit the entire world. Indeed, says Doc, in a verbatim restatement of a passage characteristic of Ricketts's thought patterns in *The Log from the Sea of Cortez,*

> The things we admire in men, kindness and generosity, openness, honesty, understanding and feeling are the concomitants of failure in our system. And those traits we detest, sharpness, greed, acquisitiveness, meanness, egotism and self-interest are the traits of success. And while men admire the quality of the first they love the produce of the second.

What distinguishes *Cannery Row* from *In Dubious Battle* and from nearly all of Steinbeck's earlier fiction is the novelist's implicit willingness to accept Ricketts's long-held views about the destructive nature of "that factor of civilization we call progress." Of course, Steinbeck had always waged war against shortsighted propagandists whose political schemes for change are attended by a loss of vision. But with the exception of the *Log,* in which he allowed Ricketts to express his own views on material progress, he consistently championed meaningful change and regarded Ricketts's nonteleological appreciation of what is as socially irresponsible. In *Cannery Row,* however, Steinbeck admits that the marine biologist may have been right all along; that despite the truth of Smuts's dictum that "purpose is the highest, most important activity of the free, creative mind," in America this sense of purpose has made us a nation of vipers. The one significant distinction between Steinbeck's handling of Doc Burton and his treatment of the Doc of *Cannery Row* is that whereas the novelist blames Burton for being unable to convert his insight into something of social meaning, Doc, although as set-apart a man as Burton, is never blamed at all. Unlike Burton, Doc is an heroic figure; the best that man can hope to become in the imperfect universe in which he lives.

By 1945, John Steinbeck's world had changed perceptibly. And what he saw in postwar America strongly mitigated against his lofty philosophical idealism. Returning to a fully industrialized California which could no longer be a parent to the kind of agrarian reform he posited in *The Grapes of Wrath,* a California in which the Rotarian creed had become the admired model of social behavior, Steinbeck, in his works following *Cannery Row,* not only questioned and attacked material self-interest, but even grew skeptical of man's ability to "grow beyond his work" and "emerge ahead of his accomplishments."

Ironically, Steinbeck's changing perspective is largely responsible for the inferior quality of much of his later writing. For Steinbeck's best works are distinguished by his organismically based belief in man's inherent capacity for achieving greatness of mind and deed (as an individual and as part of a moving phalanx) in conjunction with a Rickettsian understanding of cosmic wholeness and a faith in man's ability to break through to a vision of this unity. When, however, the novelist became convinced of the ubiquitous nature of man's self-interested drive for material wealth, Steinbeck the philosophical visionary gradually became either Steinbeck the conventional moralist exhorting man to choose goodness over evil, or Steinbeck the wasteland prophet lamenting the inevitable demise of the good man in a corrupt world.

Among Steinbeck's more adroit examinations of human nature in the context of his growing conviction about the ever-increasing nature of man's pursuit of wealth and power is *The Pearl.* Based upon a story he had heard during his expedition with Ricketts to the Gulf of California about a poor Mexican fisherman who found a fabulous pearl which he thought would guarantee his future happiness, but which almost destroyed him before he threw it back into the sea, Steinbeck worked hard on this fable, rewriting it several times. It was finally published in 1947, but went largely unnoticed, and it was not until six years later that the novelist cautiously affirmed that *The Pearl* was finally "gathering some friends."

In contrast with the bawdiness of *Cannery Row, The Pearl* is a simple, lyrical tale which Steinbeck called "a black and white story like a parable." It is a parable about the search for happiness and the nature of man's need to choose between the inherently benign natural life and the frantic, self-oriented modern world. At the crux of Steinbeck's theme in *The Pearl,* however, is not only a statement about the choice between simplicity and luxury, but also his conviction that human nature makes it impossible for man to choose what Ricketts called "the region of inward adjustments" (characterized by "friendship, tolerance, dignity, or love") until he has attempted to succeed in "the region of outward possessions." At the end of *The Pearl,* Kino, the poor fisherman, realizes the destructive nature of material wealth and hurls the pearl back into the Sea of Cortez, but Steinbeck simultaneously shows his inability to make this decision until his drive for wealth and status has ended in tragedy and disappointment. For unlike Ricketts, who believed that the simple Indians of the Gulf would disparage the quest for material wealth if untouched by the greed of their northern neighbors, Steinbeck writes in *The Pearl* that "humans are never satisfied, that you give them one thing and they want something more." And he insists, paradoxically, that this "is one of the greatest talents the species has and one that has made it superior to animals that are satisfied with what they have." *The Pearl* is Steinbeck's parable of the human dilemma; it is a study of the agony involved in man's recognition of the vanity of human wishes.

At the beginning of Steinbeck's fable, Kino is a poor but mildly satisfied pearl fisherman. A devoted husband and father, his song is the "Song of the Family," which rises "to an aching chord that caught the throat, saying this is safety, this is warmth, this is the *Whole.*" He is a man who, like the contented Indians of the Gulf depicted by Ricketts in his Sea of Cortez journal, enjoys a "deep participation with all things, the gift he had from his people."

> He heard every little sound of the gathering night, the sleepy complaint of settling birds, the love agony of cats, the strike and withdrawl of little waves on the beach, and the simple hiss of distance. And he could smell the sharp odor of exposed kelp from the receding tide.

But despite his sense of participation with the land and with his family, Kino is victimized by his poverty and exploited because of his ignorance. "He was trapped as his people were always trapped and would be until . . . they could be sure that the things in the books were really in the books." When, therefore, Kino finds "the pearl of the world," he sees in it an end to the poverty and exploitation which heretofore he has been forced to accept. Gradually, the "Song of the Pearl" merges with the "Song of the Family," Steinbeck points out, "so that the one beautified the other." And Kino envisages a day when he will be able to afford to send his child to school so that "one of his own people could tell him the truth of things." Kino tells his wife, Juana, "This is our one chance. Our son must go to school. He must break out of the pot that holds us in."

But Kino's thinking about the future becomes cloudy; his vision becomes as hazy as the mirage of the Gulf. "There was no certainty in seeing, no proof that what you saw was there or was not there." And Kino looks down into the surface of his fabulous pearl and forms misty, insubstantial dreams that will never come true. For "in this Gulf of uncertain light there were more illusions than realities."

As a member of a village of pearl fishermen, Kino is a member-unit in the organism of the greater community of La Paz. Steinbeck describes the town organismically as a "thing like a colonial animal. A town has a nervous system and a head and shoulders and feet. A town is a thing separate from all other towns, so that there are not two towns alike. And a town has a whole emotion." Thus, when Kino finds his great pearl, the organism of the town stirs to life and an interest develops in Kino—"people with things to sell and people with favors to ask."

> The essence of pearl mixed with essence of men and a curious dark residue was precipitated. Every man suddenly became related to Kino's pearl, and Kino's pearl went into the dreams, the speculations, the schemes, the plans, the futures, the wishes, the needs, the lusts, the hungers, of everyone, and only one person stood in the way and that was Kino, so that he became curiously every man's enemy.

No one resented Kino as long as he was an impoverished fisherman. But Kino stirred the fantasies of the townspeople, and upset the equilibrium of the organism.

> If every single man and woman, child and baby, acts and conducts itself in a known pattern and breaks no walls and differs with no one and experiments in no way and is not sick and does not endanger the ease and peace of mind or steady unbroken flow of the town, then that unit can disappear and never be heard of. But let one man step out of the regular thought or the known and trusted pattern, and the nerves of the townspeople ring with nervousness and communication travels over the nerve lines of the town. Then every unit communicates to the whole.

When he senses the greed of the envious villagers, Kino, who "had broken through the horizons into a cold and lonely outside" (Steinbeck's choice of words is significant here), hardens and "his eyes and his voice were hard and cold and a brooding hate was growing in him." And as attempts are made first to cheat him of his wealth and later to steal his pearl, the "Song of the Pearl" becomes a "Song of Evil" as Kino fights to save himself, his family, and his newfound wealth. Kino admits that "This pearl has become my soul. . . . If I give it up I shall lose my soul."

Gradually, Kino realizes that while he has irrevocably lost one world, he has not gained another. He insists that because "I am a man," "I will fight this thing" and "win over it," and he drives "his strength against a mountain" and plunges "against the sea." But Kino's hopes are destroyed, for as Juana, his ostensibly suppliant but strong and knowing wife (like Ma Joad, Juana is "pure Briffault"), realizes, "the mountain would stand while the man broke himself"; "the sea would surge while the man drowned in it." At the same time, Juana knows that it is the striving that makes Kino a man, "half insane and half god, and Juana had need of a man."

Kino saves his pearl from those who would steal it, but he pays dearly for it with the destruction of his house and canoe, and ultimately with the death of his baby. Finally, Kino begins to see the pearl as a "grey, malignant growth," and he chooses the "region of inward adjustments" over the "region of outward possessions" by throwing the pearl back into the Gulf. And though he has lost his canoe, his home, and his child, and so is even poorer than before, his choice has been made possible only because he has "gone through the pain" and "come out on the other side." Kino's story is the parable of the human condition; a parable of that two-legged paradox, man, growing accustomed to "the tragic miracle of consciousness," struggling, and finally succeeding, to forge the design of his microcosmic history.

While Ricketts's ideas about the inherent virtues of the simple, natural life serve as a thematic substratum on which Steinbeck builds his parable, the novelist's chief concern in *The Pearl* is with how man's failure to "participate" in "the region of inward adjustments" can lead to complete personal and social disintegration. In his next novel, *The Wayward Bus* (1947), Steinbeck moves even further from Ricketts's patterns of thought to probe the effects of materialistic self-interest on a widely diverse group of individuals, related only in that they are all victims of the self-centeredness which, for Steinbeck, more than anything else characterized the power drives in postwar American society.

The Wayward Bus is an allegory of modern life in which a random collection of men and women on a bus bound from one main California highway to another, are forced to reexamine their own lives and inspect the manner in which they interact with their fellow men. During the course of their trouble-filled journey, they destroy or at least partly redeem themselves, as they attempt or refuse to redefine their thinking and rechannel their behavior.

Thematically, the impact of Ricketts's world-view on *The Wayward Bus* is negligible. On the other hand, early in the novel Steinbeck does employ the marine biologist's unique manner of seeing as fictional method in a way he had not done since *Of Mice and Men.* In his story of Juan Chicoy and the eight passengers on his bus (named Sweetheart) bound from Juan's cafe at Rebel Corners to San Juan de la Cruz, the novelist delineates his characters with the objectivity of a scientist studying bugs under a microscope. Unlike *The Pearl,* in which Steinbeck exhibits compassion for Kino's plight, and in contrast with *Cannery Row,* where he stirs his readers' emotions with his gentle portraits of Doc and Mack's group of vagabonds, Steinbeck feels little warmth for Juan and his fellow travelers, who are consistently involved in absurd struggles, trivial power plays, and foolish self-deceptions.

As Antonia Seixas points out [in *Steinbeck and His Critics,* edited by E. W. Tedlock, Jr., and C. V. Wicker], the characters in *The Wayward Bus* are all "type-specimens," components as well as products of our civilization.

> Elliot Pritchard is the type-specimen business man; his wife, Bernice, is the type-specimen "Lady," sweet, gentle, and terribly powerful, with the unconscious craftiness of the weak and lazy who must live by rules and force those rules on all around them. There is Horton, the traveling salesman, whose best-selling item is the "Little Wonder Artificial Sore Foot." There are the adolescents, Pimples Carson, apprentice mechanic, and Norma, the homely, pathetic waitress.

But while Steinbeck describes the flawed lives of his main characters in objective detail, he never says how or why they got that way. In other words, he seems to be saying, "Here is a typical group of *homo Americanus.* See, this is how they look, this is how they act."

At this point, however, the similarity between Ricketts's objective, nonteleological way of seeing and Steinbeck's pattern of fictional reality ceases. For while Steinbeck may be more interested in how his type-specimens look and act than in their respective pasts, he is deeply concerned about their futures. In short, what begins as a nonteleological account of something that happened turns into a conventional morality play (the novel's epigraph is a quotation from *Everyman*) in which Steinbeck, an-

gered by men and women who are unconcerned with the lives of their
fellow men and who have cut themselves off from any meaningful contact
with the "region of inward adjustments," specifically structures the allegorical pattern of the novel in order to drive Sweetheart's driver and
passengers to penitence.

Since most of the novel's action takes place in and around Juan
Chicoy's bus, it is tempting to regard Sweetheart as an organism, the
constituent parts of which are Juan and his passengers. But from the
outset, Juan and the other travelers are such self-interested people leading
such fragmented lives that they are unable and unwilling to key-into their
organismic sphere of being. In contrast with this self-directed group of
"pilgrims," Steinbeck creates as a backdrop a lush and fertile nature, the
beauty of which only the most insensitive can ignore.

> In the deep spring when the grass was green on fields and
> foothills, when the lupines and poppies made a splendid blue
> and gold earth, when the great trees awakened in yellow-green
> young leaves, then there was no more lovely place in the world.
> It was no beauty you could ignore by being used to it. It caught
> you in the throat in the morning and made a pain of pleasure
> in the pit of your stomach when the sun went down over it.
> The sweet smell of the lupines and of the grass set you breath-
> ing nervously, set you panting almost sexually. And it was in
> this season of flowering and growth, though it was still before
> daylight, that Juan Chicoy came out to the bus carrying an
> electric lantern. Pimples Carson, his apprentice-mechanic, stum-
> bled sleepily behind.

Juan and Pimples (and the other wayward travelers) "stumble sleep-
ily" through life and disdain not only their fellow passengers but also the
beauty of the natural order. The characters' struggles with themselves and
with each other multiply; tensions erupt into near-violence. And the "little
wind" that blows in the passengers' faces, bringing "the smell of lupine
and the smell of a quickening earth, frantic with production" goes unnoticed.

During the journey to San Juan de la Cruz, Sweetheart is detoured off
the main highway by high floodwaters which have washed out a bridge
spanning the San Ysidro River. Here Steinbeck fuses his Everyman allegory with the Old Testament Flood motif in that events which occur along
the seldom-used and dangerous back road to San Juan force Sweetheart's
driver and passengers to reexamine themselves and reassess their relationships with their fellow travelers.

When Juan, who for some time had been trying to find a way to abandon his passengers, allows Sweetheart to swerve into a ditch, the irritable travelers step off the bus below a tall yellow cliff. As they look up, they see at the very top "in great faint letters . . . the single word REPENT. It must have been a long and dangerous job for some wild creature to put it there with black paint, and it was nearly gone now." The travelers climb to shelter in "three deep, dark caves" in the cliff below the sign, and it is in these caves that Steinbeck's Everyman theme is worked out. Deprived of all material comforts and without their driver, who has ostensibly gone to seek help, the passengers face themselves and one another squarely for the first time in the novel.

Seven of Juan's passengers undergo measurable alterations of character. All but the pernicious Mr. Van Brunt (who refuses to repent and dies in his own darkness) arrive at a somewhat fuller self-understanding and a recognition of their responsibilities toward their fellow "pilgrims." Juan Chicoy's shift in outlook is the most dramatic. Juan, who fled from the bus to an abandoned barn, suddenly gives up his illusory dream of escaping to the hills of Mexico. He returns, rallies his charges, and together, they dig Sweetheart out of the mud and travel on toward San Juan de la Cruz. As the bus resumes its journey, the passengers peer out the windows and see "a little rim of lighter sky around the edge of a great dark cloud over the western mountains." The rain clouds lift, and the evening star comes into view, shining "clear and washed and steady" on a renewed earth.

Steinbeck's Everyman allegory is simply not believable. His portrayal of nature (as in *The Moon Is Down*) is too schematic, and his characters are flat and one-dimensional. Most importantly, their repentances seem facile and essentially meaningless. Juan does come back to dig Sweetheart out of the mud. But his return is not marked by any genuine sense of commitment, but rather by a vague feeling of involvement which really amounts to little more than resignation. In short, *The Wayward Bus* is a weak novel because Steinbeck all but abandons the broad ecological and organismal substructure which gave the actions of such characters as Jim Casy, Tom Joad, and even Mayor Orden and Kino, a genuine locus of meaning. There is no character, who, by breaking through to a knowledge of the deep thing, makes the "education of the heart" philosophically satisfying. Sweetheart lumbers on into San Juan, but one feels that the passengers, though momentarily shaken from their petty self-interest, lack any sense of purpose and so will return to the hypocritical beliefs and shallow dreams which characterize the world of which they are products and victims. Essentially motionless, Juan and his passengers never really key-into a moving phalanx of any kind. They do not "grow beyond their concepts" because they have no concepts. And they cannot "emerge ahead of their accomplishments" because they have accomplished little. In short, the characters in *The Wayward Bus* really do no more than the animals Steinbeck and Ricketts observed in the tide pools of the Sea of Cortez: SURVIVE. And this, the novelist seems to say, perhaps without consciously recognizing it, is the tragedy of man's wayward pilgrimage through the wasteland of modern life.

In late May 1951, while Steinbeck was hard at work on *East of Eden,* he reflected back a few years and noted that before he met his wife Elaine and started serious work on his new novel, "every life force was shriveling. Work was nonexistent. I remember it very well. The wounds were gangrenous and mostly I just didn't give a dam[n]." Steinbeck's early postwar fiction reflects the growing infection which led to these gangrenous wounds. The novelist had returned from the war to a vastly changed America. He tried first (in *Cannery Row*) to recapture a sense of the past, only to realize that neither the dropout nor the scientific-philosophic visionary could long survive the onslaught of civilization. Then, in *The Pearl,* he employed an old legend to explain the modern dilemma of man's drive to better himself and the concomitant woe which attends the craving. Finally, in *The Wayward Bus,* Steinbeck focused directly on the specimen-types who people the modern world and attempted with little artistic success to drive these characters to penitence.

Gradually, Steinbeck was becoming a novelist without a vision. His organismic view of man and the world, and his belief in the manner in which individuals can key-into a moving phalanx to work toward common human goals seemed increasingly ludicrous in a society of splintered, self-directed Americans. Simultaneously, Steinbeck apparently became convinced that Ricketts's understanding of the deep thing, of the fundamental unity of all life in a cosmic whole was meaningless in a world in which most men and women were too preoccupied with their own interests to seek that knowledge. Most importantly, *The Pearl* and *The Wayward Bus* are Steinbeck's first full-length works in a decade in which there are no Ricketts philosopher-figures whose ideas help to directly voice or ironically reflect that unique view of man and the cosmos which characterizes the novelist's greatest writing.

HOWARD LEVANT

The Fully Matured Art:
The Grapes of Wrath

The enormous contemporary social impact of *The Grapes of Wrath* can encourage the slippery reasoning that condemns a period novel to die with its period. But continuing sales and critical discussions suggest that *The Grapes of Wrath* has outlived its directly reportorial ties to the historical past; that it can be considered as an aesthetic object, a good or a bad novel *per se*. In that light, the important consideration is the relative harmony of its structure and materials.

The Grapes of Wrath is an attempted prose epic, a summation of national experience at a given time. Evaluation proceeds from that identification of genre. A negative critical trend asserts that *The Grapes of Wrath* is too flawed to command serious attention: The materials are local and temporary, not universal and permanent; the conception of life is overly simple; the characters are superficial types (except, perhaps, Ma Joad); the language is folksy or strained by turns; and, in particular, the incoherent structure is the weakest point—the story breaks in half, the nonorganic, editorializing interchapters force unearned general conclusions, and the ending is inconclusive as well as overwrought and sentimental. The positive trend asserts that *The Grapes of Wrath* is a great novel. Its materials are properly universalized in specific detail; the conception is philosophical; the characters are warmly felt and deeply created; the language is functional, varied, and superb on the whole; and the structure is an almost perfect combination of the dramatic and the panoramic in sufficient har-

From *The Novels of John Steinbeck: A Critical Study*. © 1974 by the Curators of the University of Missouri. University of Missouri Press, 1974.

mony with the materials. This criticism admits that overwrought idealistic passages as well as propagandistic simplifications turn up on occasion, but these are minor flaws in an achievement on an extraordinary scale. Relatively detached studies of Steinbeck's ideas comprise a third trend. These studies are not directly useful in analytical criticism; they do establish that Steinbeck's social ideas are ordered and legitimate extensions of biological fact, hence scientific and true rather than mistaken or sentimental.

The two evaluative positions are remarkable in their opposition. They are perhaps overly simple in asserting that *The Grapes of Wrath* is either a classic of our literature or a formless pandering to sentimental popular taste. Certainly these extremes are mistaken in implying (when they do) that, somehow, *The Grapes of Wrath* is *sui generis* in relation to Steinbeck's work.

Trends so awkwardly triple need to be brought into a sharper focus. By way of a recapitulation in focus, consider a few words of outright praise:

> For all of its sprawling asides and extravagances, *The Grapes of Wrath* is a big book, a great book, and one of maybe two or three American novels in a class with *Huckleberry Finn*.

Freeman Champney's praise is conventional enough to pass unquestioned if one admires *The Grapes of Wrath,* or, if one does not, it can seem an invidious borrowing of prestige, shrilly emotive at that. Afterthought emphasizes the serious qualification of the very high praise. Just how much damage is wrought by those "sprawling asides and extravagances," and does *The Grapes of Wrath* survive its structural faults as *Huckleberry Finn* does, by virtue of its mythology, its characterization, its language? If the answers remain obscure, illumination may increase (permitting, as well, a clearer definition of the aesthetic efficacy of Steinbeck's ideas) when the context of critical discussion is the relationship of the novel's structure to its materials.

Steinbeck's serious intentions and his artistic honesty are not in question. He had studied and experienced the materials intensely over a period of time. After a false start that he rejected (*L'Affaire Lettuceburg*), his conscious intention was to create an important literary work rather than a propagandistic shocker or a journalistic statement of the topical problem of how certain people faced one aspect of the Great Depression. Therefore, it is an insult to Steinbeck's aims to suggest that somehow *The Grapes of Wrath* is imperfect art but a "big" or "great" novel nevertheless. In all critical justice, *The Grapes of Wrath* must stand or fall as a serious and important work of art.

The consciously functional aspect of Steinbeck's intentions—his working of the materials—is clarified by a comparison of *The Grapes of Wrath* with *In Dubious Battle*. Both novels deal with labor problems peculiar to California, but that similarity cannot be pushed too far. The Joads are fruit pickers in California, but not of apples, the fruit mentioned in *In Dubious Battle*. The Joads pick cotton, and in the strike novel the people expect to move on to cotton. The Joads become involved in a strike but as strikebreakers rather than as strikers. Attitudes are less easy to camouflage. The strikers in *In Dubious Battle* and the Okies in *The Grapes of Wrath* are presented with sympathy whereas the owning class and much of the middle class have no saving virtue. The sharpest similarity is that both the strikers and the Okies derive a consciousness of the need for group action from their experiences; but even here there is a difference in emphasis. The conflict of interest is more pointed and the lessons of experience are less ambiguous in *The Grapes of Wrath* than in *In Dubious Battle*. The fact is that the two novels are not similar beyond a common basis in California labor problems, and Steinbeck differentiates that basis carefully in most specific details. The really significant factor is that different structures are appropriate to each novel. The restricted scope of *In Dubious Battle* demands a dramatic structure with some panoramic elements as they are needed. The broad scope of *The Grapes of Wrath* demands a panoramic structure; the dramatic elements appear as they are needed. Therefore, in each case, the primary critical concern must be the adequacy of the use of the materials, not the materials in themselves.

Steinbeck's profound respect for the materials of *The Grapes of Wrath* is recorded in a remarkable letter in which he explained to his literary agents and to his publisher the main reason for his withdrawing *L'Affaire Lettuceburg,* the hurried, propagandistic, thirty-thousand-word manuscript novel that preceded *The Grapes of Wrath*:

> I know I promised this book to you, and that I am breaking a promise in withholding it. But I had got smart and cagey you see. I had forgotten that I hadn't learned to write books, that I will never learn to write them. A book must be a life that lives all of itself and this one doesn't do that. You can't write a book. It isn't that simple. The process is more painful than that. And this book is fairly clever, has skillful passages, but tricks and jokes. Sometimes I, the writer, seem a hell of a smart guy—just twisting this people out of shape. But the hell with it. I beat poverty for a good many years and I'll be damned if I'll go

down at the first little whiff of success. I hope you, Pat, don't think I've double-crossed you. In the long run to let this book out would be to double-cross you. But to let the bars down is like a first theft. It's hard to do, but the second time it isn't so hard and pretty soon it is easy. If I should write three books like this and let them out, I would forget there were any other kinds.

This is Steinbeck's declaration of artistic purpose—and his effort to exorcise a dangerous (and permanent) aspect of his craft. Much of the motivation for Steinbeck's career is stated in this letter. After all, he did write *L'Affaire Lettuceburg*; and "tricks and jokes," detached episodes, and detached ironic hits, as well as a twisting of characters, are evident enough in much of Steinbeck's earlier work. But the Depression materials were too serious to treat lightly or abstractly, or to subject to an imposed structure (mistaken idealism, nature worship, a metaphysical curse, a literary parallel). Such materials need to be in harmony with an appropriate structure.

From that intentional perspective, the central artistic problem is to present the universal and epical in terms of the individual and particular. Steinbeck chooses to deal with this by creating an individual, particular image of the epical experience of the dispossessed Okies by focusing a sustained attention on the experience of the Joads. The result is an organic combination of structures. Dramatic structure suits the family's particular history; panoramic structure proves out the representative nature of their history. To avoid a forced and artificial "typing," to assure that extensions of particular detail are genuinely organic, Steinbeck postulates a conceptual theme that orders structure and materials: the transformation of the Joad family from a self-contained, self-sustaining unit to a conscious part of a group, a whole larger than its parts. This thematic ordering is not merely implicit or ironic, as it is in *The Pastures of Heaven,* or withheld to create mystery as in *Cup of Gold* or *To a God Unknown*. Steinbeck chances the strength of the materials and the organic quality of their structure. And he defines differences: The group is not group-man. The earlier concept is a "beast," created by raw emotion ("blood"), short-lived, unwieldly, unpredictable, mindless; a monster that produces indiscriminate good or evil. The group is quite different—rational, stable, relatively calm—because it is an assemblage of like-minded people who retain their individual and traditional sense of right and wrong as a natural fact. Group-man lacks a moral dimension; the group is a morally pure instrument of power. The difference is acute at the level of leadership. The leaders have ambiguous aims in *In Dubious Battle,* but they are Christ-like (Jim Casy) or attain moral insight (Tom Joad) in *The Grapes of Wrath.*

The Grapes of Wrath is optimistic; *In Dubious Battle* is not. That the living part of the Joad family survives, though on the edge of survival, is less than glowingly optimistic, but that survival produces a mood that differs considerably from the unrelenting misery of *In Dubious Battle.* Optimism stems from the theme, most openly in the alternation of narrative chapter and editorial interchapter. While the Joads move slowly and painfully toward acceptance of the group, many of the interchapters define the broad necessity of that acceptance. Arbitrary plotting does not produce this change. Its development is localized in Ma Joad's intense focus on the family's desire to remain a unit; her recognition of the group is the dramatic resolution. ("Use' ta be the fambly was fust. It ain't so now. It's anybody. Worse off we get, the more we got to do.") Optimism is demonstrated also in experience that toughens, educates, and enlarges the stronger Joads in a natural process. On the simplest, crudest level, the family's journey and ordeal is a circumstantial narrative of an effort to reach for the good material life. Yet that is not the sole motive, and those members who have only that motive leave the family. On a deeper level, the family is attempting to rediscover the identity it lost when it was dispossessed; so the Joads travel from order (their old, traditional life) through disorder (the road, California) to some hope of a better, rediscovered order, which they reach in Ma's recognition and Tom's dedication. Their journey toward order is the ultimate optimistic, ennobling process, the earned, thematic resolution of the novel.

I do not intend to imply that Steinbeck pretties his materials. He does not stint the details of the family's various privations, its continual losses of dignity, and the death or disappearance of many of its members. On the larger scale, there is considerable objective documentation of the general economic causes of such misery—a circumstantial process that lifts *The Grapes of Wrath* out of the merely historic genre of the proletarian novel. Optimism survives as the ultimate value because of the will of the people to understand and to control the conditions of their lives despite constant discouragement.

This value is essentially abstract, political. Steinbeck deepens and universalizes it by developing the relationship between the family unit and "the people." The family is made up of unique individuals. "The people" embraces a timeless entity, a continuing past, present, and future of collective memory—but free of any social or political function. Time-lag confounds the usefulness of "the people" as a guide for the present. The Joads and others like them know they may keep the land or get new land if they can kill or control "the Bank," as the old people killed Indians to take the land and controlled nature to keep it. But "the Bank" is more complicated an enemy than Indians or nature because it is an abstraction. (That buccaneering capitalism is an abstract or allegorical monster of evil is left to implication in *In Dubious Battle*. Steinbeck is far more directly allegorical in characterizing "the Bank" as an evil, nonhuman monster. Consequently there is, I think, a gain in horror but a relative loss of credibility.) So the Okies submit to dispossession in Oklahoma (forced by mechanized cheaper production of cotton) and to the huge migration into California (encouraged by landowners to get cheap field labor), motivated by the time-lag that confuses them, for none of them comprehends the monstrous logic of modern economics. Despite their ignorance, in a process that is unifying in itself and is second only to survival, the families work at some way of prevailing against "the Bank." The older, agrarian concept of "the people" is succeeded in time by the new concept of the group, an instrument of technology and political power—an analogue that works. Steinbeck makes this succession appear necessary and legitimate by a representation that excludes alternate solutions. The permitted solution seems a natural evolution, from people to group, because it is a tactic, not a fundamental change in folkways. Its process is long and painful because the emotive entity, "the people," needs to feel its way toward redefinition as the group—the abstract, political entity which emerges as an organic, particularized whole. This is brilliant literary strategy, in its grasp of operative metaphor and its avoidance of an overly obvious, loaded opposition. Steinbeck is scrupulously careful to keep to precise and exact circumstantial detail in this developed metaphor. Concretely, the panicky violence of "the Bank" is the reverse of the fact that (seemingly by habit) the Joads are kind to those who need their help and neighborly to people who are like them. The metaphor is persuasive.

Steinbeck is quite as scrupulous in the use of allegory as a way of universalizing an abstract particular. In his earlier work this method can produce a tangibly artificial, forced result, but allegory is a credible and functional device in *The Grapes of Wrath*. The turtle episode in chapter 3 is justly famous. Objectively, we have a fully realized description of a land turtle's patient, difficult journey over dust fields, across a road and walled embankment, and on through the dust. The facts are the starting point; nature is not distorted or manipulated to yield allegorical meaning. The turtle seems awkward but it is able to survive, like the Joads, and like them it is moving southwest, out of the dry area. It can protect itself against a natural danger like the red ant it kills, as the Joads protect themselves by their unity. The turtle's eyes are "fierce, humorous," suggesting force that takes itself easily; the stronger Joads are a fierce, humorous people. When mismanaged human power attacks, as when a truck swerves to hit the turtle, luck is on the animal's side—it survives by luck. The Joads survive the mismanagement that produced the Dust Bowl and the brutalizing man-made conditions in California as much by luck as by design. The relation to the Joads of the life-bearing function of the turtle is more obscure, or perhaps overly ambitious. The factual starting point is that, unknowingly, the turtle carries an oat seed in its shell and unknowingly drops and plants the seed in the dust, where it will rest until water returns. The most obvious link in the Joad family is the pregnant Rose of Sharon, but her baby is born dead. Perhaps compassion is "born," as in Uncle John's thoughts as he floats the dead baby down the flooding river in its apple box coffin:

> Go down an' tell 'em. Go down in the street an' rot an' tell 'em that way. That's the way you can talk. . . . Maybe they'll know then. (The reversal of values is evident in the reversed symbolism; the river bears death—not life, the coffin—not water to seeds in the earth.)

But this appeal is strained, too greatly distanced from the factual starting point. The link works in the restricted sense that Ruthie and Winfield are "planted," and will perhaps take root, in the new environment of California. At this point the careful allegory collapses under its own weight, yet care is taken to join the device to the central narrative. In chapter 4, Tom Joad picks up a turtle, and later Casy remarks on the tenacity of the breed:

> "Nobody can't keep a turtle though. They work at it and work at it, and at last one day they get out and away they go—off somewheres."

This recognition of the turtle's purposeful tenacity interprets and places the preceding interchapter in the central narrative. Tom calls the turtle "an old bulldozer," a figure that works in opposition to the threatening insect life the tractors suggest as self-defeating, destructive tools of "the Bank." Again, a purposeful turtle is opposed to homeless domestic animals, like the "thick-furred yellow shepherd dog" that passes Tom and Casy, to suggest precisely the ruined land and the destruction of the old ways of life on the most basic, animal level, where the wild (or free) animal survives best. These and other supporting details extend the exemplum into the narrative; they continue and deepen Steinbeck's foreshadowing, moralizing insight naturally, within the range of biological imagery. It is true, allowing for the one collapse of the allegory, that none of Steinbeck's earlier work exhibits as profound a comprehension of what can be done to "place" an allegorical narrative device.

The turtle interchapter is masterful enough. Steinbeck does even more with an extended instance of allegorizing—the introduction of the lapsed preacher, Jim Casy, into the Joad family. Casy has a role that is difficult to present within the limits of credibility. Casy may look too much like his function, the Christ-like force that impels the family toward its transformation into the group. If the novel is to have more significance than a reportorial narrative of travel and hardship, Casy's spiritual insights are a necessary means of stating a convincing philosophical optimism. The technical difficulty is that Casy does not have a forthright narrative function. He drops out of the narrative for almost one hundred and fifty pages, although his presence continues through the Joads' wondering at times what had happened to him. When he reenters the novel, he is killed off within fifteen pages—sacrificed for the group in accord with his Christ-like function, with a phrase that recalls Christ's last words. In spite of the obvious technical difficulty in handling such materials, Steinbeck realizes Casy as fully as any of the major Joads. Casy's struggle with himself to define "sin" to include the necessary facts of the natural world lends him a completely human aspect. He earns the right to make moral statements because he bases all judgments on his own experience. This earned right to "witness" serves to keep Casy human, yet it permits him to function as if he were an allegorical figure. This is a brilliant solution, and Casy is Steinbeck's most successful use of a functional allegorical figure in a major role. His narrative sharpness contrasts amazingly with the dim realization of Sir Henry Morgan or Joseph Wayne.

Even Casy's necessary distance is functional rather than arbitrary. He exists outside the narrative in the sense that he travels with the Joads but he is not a member of the family, and there is no danger of confusing his adventures with theirs. Further, by right of his nature and experience, he has the function of being the living moral conscience of "the people." He travels with the Joads to witness the ordeal of the Okies, to understand its causes, and to do what he can to help. Steinbeck's convincing final touch is that, at the end, Tom Joad aspires to Casy's role. In this shift, Steinbeck manipulates allegory, he does not submit to its rigid quality, for Tom is not like Casy. Tom is far more violent, more capable of anger; having been shown the way, however, he may be more successful as a practical missionary than Casy. One might say that if Casy is to be identified with Christ, the almost human god, Tom is to be identified with Saint Paul, the realistic, tough organizer. The allegorical link by which Tom is "converted" and assumes Casy's role is deeply realized and rich with significance, not simply because it is a technical necessity, but because it is a confirmation of Casy's reality as a man and a teacher. The parallels to Christ and Saint Paul would be only arid technical facts if they were not realized so profoundly. The trivial fact that Casy has Christ's initials dims beside this more profound and sustained realization.

Function, not mere design, is as evident in the use of characterization to support and develop a conflict of opposed ideas—mainly a struggle between law and anarchy. The one idea postulates justice in a moral world of love and work, identified in the past with "the people" and in the present with the government camp and finally with the union movement, since these are the modern, institutional forms the group may take. The opposed idea postulates injustice in an immoral world of hatred and starvation. It is associated with buccaneering capitalism, which, in violent form, includes strikebreaking and related practices that cheapen human labor.

The Joads present special difficulties in characterization. They must be individualized to be credible and universalized to carry out their representative functions. Steinbeck meets these problems by making each of the Joads a specific individual and by specifying that what happens to the Joads is typical of the times. The means he uses to maintain these identities can be shown in some detail. The least important Joads are given highly specific tags—Grandma's religion, Grandpa's vigor, Uncle John's melancholy, and Al's love of cars and girls. The tags are involved in events; they are not inert labels. Grandma's burial violates her religion; Grandpa's vigor ends when he leaves the land; Uncle John's melancholy balances the family's experience; Al helps to drive the family to California and, by marrying, continues the family. Ma, Pa, Rose of Sharon, and Tom carry the narrative, so their individuality is defined by events rather than through events. Ma is the psychological and moral center of the family; Pa carries its burdens; Rose of Sharon means to ensure its physical continuity; and Tom becomes its moral conscience. On the larger scale, there is much evidence that what happens to the family is typical of the times. The interchapters pile up suggestions that "the whole country is moving" or about to move. The Joads meet many of their counterparts or outsiders who are in sympathy with their ordeal; these meetings reenforce the common bond of "the people." Both in the interchapters and the narrative, the universal, immediate issue is survival—a concrete universal.

On the other hand, the individualized credibility of the Joads is itself
the source of two difficulties: the Joads are too different, as sharecroppers,
to suggest a universal or even a national woe, and they speak an argot that
might limit their universal quality. (It is a curious fact that Steinbeck
attempts to create a so-called "universal language" in *Burning Bright,* a far
more theory-ridden novel than *The Grapes of Wrath.* In any event, the
attempt produces a fantastic, wholly incredible language.) Steinbeck han-
dles these limitations with artistic license. The narrative background contains the Joads' past; their experience as a landless proletariat is highlighted
in the narrative foreground. The argot is made to seem a typical language
within the novel in three ways: It is the major language; people who are
not Okies speak variations of their argot; and that argot is not specialized
in its relevance, but is used to communicate the new experiences "the
people" have in common as a landless proletariat. However, because these
solutions depend on artistic license, any tonal falseness undermines severely the massive artistic truthfulness the language is intended to present.
So the overly editorial tone in several of the interchapters has a profoundly
false linguistic ring, although the tonal lapse is limited and fairly trivial in
itself.

The Joads are characterized further in comparison with four Okie
types who refuse to know or are unable to gain the knowledge the family
derives from its collective experience. They are the stubborn, the dead, the
weak, and the backtrackers; they appear in the novel in that order.

Muley Graves is the stubborn man, as his punning name suggests. He
reveals himself to Tom and Casy near the beginning of the novel. His
refusal to leave Oklahoma is mere stubbornness; his isolation drives him
somewhat mad. He is aware of a loss of reality, of "jus' wanderin' aroun'
like a damn ol' graveyard ghos'," and his blind violence is rejected from
the beginning by the strongest, who oppose his pessimism with an essential
optimism.

Deaths of the aged and the unborn frame the novel. Grandpa and
Grandma are torn up by the roots and die, incapable of absorbing a new,
terrible experience. Rose of Sharon's baby, born dead at the end of the
novel, is an index of the family's ordeal and a somewhat contrived symbol
of the necessity to form the group.

The weak include two extremes within the Joad family. Noah Joad
gives up the struggle to survive; he finds a private peace. His character is
shadowy, and his choice is directed more clearly by Steinbeck than by any
substance within him. Connie has plenty of substance. He is married to
Rose of Sharon and deserts her because he has no faith in the family's

struggle to reach California. His faith is absorbed in the values of "the Bank," in getting on, in money, in any abstract goal. He wishes to learn about technology in order to rise in the world. He does not admire technique for itself, as Al does. He is a sexual performer, but he loves no one. Finally, he wishes that he had stayed behind in Oklahoma and taken a job driving a tractor. In short, with Connie, Steinbeck chooses brilliantly to place a "Bank" viewpoint within the family. By doing so, he precludes a simplification of character and situation, and he endorses the complexity of real people in the real world. (*In Dubious Battle* is similarly free of schematic characterization.) In addition, the family's tough, humanistic values gain in credibility by their contrast with Connie's shallow, destructive modernity. The confused gas station owner and the pathetic one-eyed junkyard helper are embodied variations on Connie's kind of weakness. Al provides an important counterpoint. He wants to leave the family at last, like Connie, but duty and love force him to stay. His hard choice points the moral survival of the family and measures its human expense.

The Joads meet several backtrackers. The Wilsons go back because Mrs. Wilson is dying; the Joads do not stop, in spite of death. The ragged man's experience foreshadows what the Joads find in California; but they keep on. Some members of the Joad family think of leaving but do not, or they leave for specific reasons—a subtle variation on backtracking. Al and Uncle John wish deeply at times to leave, but they stay; Tom leaves (as Casy does) but to serve the larger, universal family of the group. Backtracking is a metaphor, then, a denial of life, but always a fact as well. The factual metaphor is deepened into complexity because the Joads sympathize with the backtrackers' failure to endure the hardships of the road and of California, in balance with where they started from—the wasteland— while knowing they cannot accept that life-denying solution. All of these choices are the fruit of the family's experience.

A fifth group of owners and middle-class people are accorded no sympathetic comprehension, as contrasted with the Joads, and, as in *In Dubious Battle,* their simply and purely monstrous characterization is too abstract to be fully credible. The few exceptions occur in highly individualized scenes or episodes (chapter 15 is an example) in which middle-class "shitheels" are caricatures of the bad guys, limited to a broad contrast with the good guys (the truck drivers, the cook), who are in sympathy with a family of Okies. (Fifteen years later, Steinbeck detailed this technique in a witty article, "How to Tell Good Guys from Bad Guys," *The Reporter* 12 (March 10, 1955), 42–44. In that quite different, political context, Steinbeck demonstrates that he knows the technique is too bluntly black

and white to permit any but the broadest cartoon characterization. There
is every reason to think he knew as much in 1935 or 1939.) This limitation
has the narrative advantage of highlighting the importance and vitality of
the Okies to the extent that they seem by right to belong in the context of
epic materials, but the disadvantage of shallow characterization is severe.
Steinbeck can provide a convincing detailed background of the conditions
of the time; he cannot similarly give a rounded, convincing characterization to an owner or a disagreeable middle-class person.

On the whole, then, fictive strength and conviction are inherent in the
materials of *The Grapes of Wrath*. The noticeable flaws are probably
irreducible aspects of the time-context and of narrative shorthand, coun-
terpointed by a complex recognition of human variety in language and
behavior.

The ordering of the structure supports this conclusion. *The Grapes of
Wrath* has three parts: Tom's return and his witnessing of events; the
family's departure and experiences on the road; its arrival and experiences
in California. The interchapters "locate" and generalize the narrative
chapters, somewhat like stage directions. They supply, in a suitably dramatic or rhetorical style, information the Joads cannot possess, and they
are involved more often than not in the narrative. (Because of that involvement, it is incorrect to think of the interchapters as choral. We see the
difference in comparing the four detached interchapters in *Cup of Gold*
with any interchapters in *The Grapes of Wrath*, and we see as well
Steinbeck's artistic growth in the organic integration of chapter and
interchapter in the later novel. The stylistic variety always suited to its
content is further evidence of a conscious, intentional artistry.) This device
provides for both precise detail and epic scope. The imagery fulfills the
structural purpose of pitting life against death.

The first part contains ten chapters. The opening is a "location"
interchapter. The dead land of the Dust Bowl in Oklahoma provides the
imagery of a universal death, but at the close the women watch their men
to see if they will break in the stress of that natural disaster. The men do
not break; the scene is repeated in California at the close of the novel in a
rising rhetoric. The objective imagistic frame sets life against death, and
life endures in the will of the people to endure. The following nine
chapters center on Tom's return from a kind of death—prison. With Casy,
Tom is an external observer, witnessing with fresh eyes the dead land and
the universal dispossession. Death seems to prevail. The turtle interchapter
is recapitulated ironically in the narrative. Pa carries handbills that promise jobs in California, an analogue to the turtle carrying a head of oats; but

the handbills falsely promise renewal; their intention is to cheapen the labor market. Later events prove the group concept is the genuine renewal, the true goal. Immediately, death is associated with "the Bank," an abstraction presented concretely in symbolic form as the tractor—the perfect tool of the abstract "Bank," which dehumanizes its driver and kills the fertility of the land.

When he sees the abandoned Joad home, Tom says, "Maybe they're all dead," but Muley Graves tells Tom the family is alive, with Uncle John, and about to leave without him for California. Tom is reborn or returned to life within the family, but its vital center has shifted (as represented in charged, frankly mystical terms) to a life-giving machine:

> The family met at the most important place, near the truck.
> The house was dead, and the fields were dead; but this truck
> was the active thing, the living principle.

The family's certainties develop from an ironically hopeful innocence, a failure to realize that a new basis for life has overtaken them, replacing family with group. The trek is an instinctive flight from death, but the economic system is more deadly than the drouth. The Joads accept the promise of the handbills, they are cheated when they sell their farm equipment, but they do not doubt that they will transplant themselves in California. The real certainty is the death of the past, as in the burning of relics by an unnamed woman in an interchapter, and by Ma herself, just before the trek begins.

All that is not dead is altered. Pa's loss of authority to Ma and Al's new authority (he knows automobiles) represent the shifts in value within the family. They retain a living coherence as farmers. They work as a unit when they kill and salt down the hogs in preparation for the trek. They are innocent of the disgusting techniques of close dealing in business, but Tom explains to Casy how the Joads can deal closely enough in their accustomed agrarian context. Their innocence, therefore, is touching, not comic, and their literal preparations support a symbolic preparation, a blindly hopeful striving to find life. Their journey is an expression, despite all shocks and changes, of the will to survive; hence, it has an epic dignity, echoing their retained, personal dignity.

In all the imagery of life and death, Steinbeck is consistent in that his symbols grow out of objective, literal facts. He thus achieves imagery in a more fully realized texture in this novel than in earlier work. This organically realized symbolism is maintained and developed in the seven chapters of the second section.

With the dead land behind them, the family carries the death of the past on its journey. Grandpa dies on the first night. Probably his stroke is caused, at least in part, by the "medicine" that Ma and Tom dope him with to take him away from the land—for the good of the family as a whole. An incipient group concept emerges in this overriding concern for the whole. Grandpa's death is offset by the meeting of the Joads and the Wilsons. At the beginning, Grandpa's illness and death join the two families in bonds of sympathy. There are other unifying forces; the language bar becomes senseless, and the two families help each other. Casy sees the emergence of the group, the whole absorbing the individual, in his sermon for Grandpa:

> Casy said solemnly, "This here ol' man jus' lived a life an' jus' died out of it. I don't know whether he was good or bad, but that don't matter much. He was alive, an' that's what matters. An' now he's dead, an' that don't matter. Heard a fella tell a poem one time, an' he says, 'All that lives is holy.' "

A modest dignity embodies the vitalistic dogma. As a further push from individual to group, the family decides to break the law by burying Grandpa secretly beside the road; a conventional funeral would eat up the money they need to reach California. Grandma's grisly, circumstantial death is delayed until the end of the section; it outweighs the achievement of reaching their destination and foreshadows the reality of California. True, the family can absorb death, even new kinds of death, into its experience. Ruthie and Winfield react most violently to the dog's death at the first stop on the road; they are less affected by Grandpa's death, still less by Grandma's. Late on the night of Grandpa's death after the Joads and Wilsons have agreed to join forces, Ma remarks: "Grandpa—it's like he's dead a year." Experience breeds a calm in the face of loss that fills in the past. Tom points this harshly realistic network of difference after Grandma's death:

> "They was too old," he said. "They wouldn't of saw nothin' that's here. Grampa would a been a-seein' the Injuns an' the prairie country when he was a young fella. An' Granma would a remembered an' seen the first home she lived in. They was too ol'. Who's really seein' it is Ruthie and Winfiel.' "

Life matters. The narrative context supports this fruit of the family's private experience. Between the deaths of Grandpa and Grandma, the Joads meet several symbolically dead people on the road. The gas station owner is incapable of learning the meaning of his own experience even when it is explained to him. The one-eyed junkyard helper lives in a prison of self, inside his ugly face and unclean body. Tom (who was in an actual prison) tries unsuccessfully to force him from his death into life. The several returning sharecroppers have come to accept a living death as the only reality. They have cut themselves off from the inchoate struggle to form a group, admittedly against severe odds, so they have no choice but to return to the dead, empty land.

But to outsiders, seeing only the surface, the Joads are not heroic life-bearers but stupidly ignorant, as in a dialogue between two service station boys when the family leaves on the final lap of the trek, the night trip across the Mojave Desert:

> "Jesus, I'd hate to start out in a jalopy like that." "Well, you and me got sense. Them goddamn Okies got no sense and no feeling. They ain't human. A human being wouldn't live like they do. A human being couldn't stand to be so dirty and miserable. They ain't a hell of a lot better than gorillas." "Just the same, I'm glad I ain't crossing the desert in no Hudson Super-Six. . . ." "You know, they don't have much trouble. They're so goddamn dumb they don't know it's dangerous. And, Christ Almighty, they don't know any better than what they got. Why worry?"

The dialogue is exactly true, but the truth is ironic. The Joads do have the appearance of death, and ignorant, dirty, dispossessed yokels seem to be unlikely carriers of an affirmation of life. The ironic truth defines the heroism of the Joads. The family is aware of the dangers of the desert crossing, and Grandma dies during it, "for the fambly," as Ma says. In general the family is more aware than the boys at the service station are allowed to know. After meeting a second returning sharecropper, the Joads are even aware of the actual conditions in California; Uncle John, the family's weakest moral agent, voices the family's rejection of despair when he says, "We're a-goin' there, ain't we? None of this here talk gonna keep us from goin' there." The service-station boys express, so we can dismiss, a superficially sentimental view of the Joads. The ironic truth is that the family goes ahead, knowing the dangers and aware that California may not be Eden. Their genuine heroism and nobility are all the more valid for being tested by irony.

Yet there is no suggestion that the Joads are merely deterministic formulae. They are pawns of circumstance up to a point. They react to

events they do not understand fully, and no doubt partial ignorance and
pure necessity keep them on the road and get them to California. But Ma
and Tom undergo certain developments of character that exclude determinism. Ma's constantly increasing moral authority is her response to the
forces that are tearing the family apart, but she acts out of a love that is
restricted to the family, that is not universalized until very near the end of
the novel. Tom's role is more extensive and more complex. He begins by
regarding himself as a creature of necessity—"I ruther jus'——lay one foot
down in front a the other"—but his quietism relates to a prison experience he does not want to live "over an' over." His natural understanding of
why and how people behave forces him into a moral concern that is larger
but as intense as Ma's. His knowledge of people is established at the
beginning of the novel, in his shrewd, unflattering understanding of the
truck driver who gives him a lift, and it widens subsequently with experience on the road. His disdain for the gas station owner precedes his tough
moral lecture to the one-eyed junkyard helper and an equally tough lecture
to Al. That is to say, Tom is involved. His moral development follows
Casy's, with the significant difference that his is the more difficult to
achieve. Casy is a relatively simple character; he can express moral concern easily. Tom's emotional numbness following his time in prison does
not permit meditation or cancel personality, so the awakening of his moral
consciousness on the road is a more rigorous, more painful experience
than Casy's time in the desert. Consequently, because of its special quality,
Tom's growing awareness of good and evil is a highly credible mirror of
the general experience that drives the family toward the group. The logic is
paradoxical, but the artistic insight is realized deeply in Tom's circumstantial
journey from moral quietism to moral concern for the group.

Enduring all the harsh experiences of their journey, the family gains
moral stature and finds that it can function as a unit in the new environment of the road. Its survival in California is a result in part of its
redefinition gained on the road.

The interchapters underscore and generalize these particulars. Chapter
14 states the growth of the group concept as a shift in the thinking of the
migrants from *I* to *we*. The narrative context is Grandpa's death and the
unity of the Joads and Wilsons. Chapter 15 suggests that the Joads' ordeal
is a moral experience that affects society at large. Chapter 17 continues the
theme that the road furthers the growth of the group concept:

> Every night relationships that make a world, established; every
> morning the world torn down like a circus. At first the families

were timid in the building and tumbling worlds, but gradually the technique of building worlds became their technique. Then leaders emerged, then laws were made, then codes came into being. And as the worlds moved westward they were more complete and better furnished, for their builders were more experienced in building them.

The formation of a group is a "technique" with its basis in the older agrarian order. As with the Joads, the experience of building produces a new moral stature and a redefinition of the family.

In the relation of these events and changes, the narrative chapters and interchapters cohere in an organic unity. Their common theme is movement from and through death to a new life inherent in the group concept. The symbolic level extends the narrative level of movement on the road through time and space. The texture is fully realized. No generalization violates narrative particulars or exists apart from them. Steinbeck's work is careful, convincing, flawless.

The third part—the family's arrival and experience in California— marks an artistic decline. The materials alter and at times the structure is defective.

The chief difference in the materials is an absolute focus on man-made misery. In Oklahoma and on the road, survival can seem to be mainly a struggle against natural conditions. Drouth is the cause of the migration. "The Bank" dispossesses the Okies, but it is not the effective cause of the drouth. In California the struggle is almost entirely against men, and there is no possibility of an escape by further migration. The chief difference in structure stems from Steinbeck's need to begin to think of how to conclude the novel, which presents structural choices and manipulations not present in the first two parts of the novel. For a time the narrative thrust remains coherent, an organic unity disguising these changes.

Grandma's undignified burial establishes the pattern of the family's experience in California. Her pauper's funeral by the state contrasts with the full dignity and free will the family expressed in burying Grandpa. Landless poverty is a moral insult to family pride, and it affects their will to survive. For the moment, as their moral spokesman, Ma expresses a will to recover as quickly as possible for the sake of the future:

> "We got to git," she said. "We got to find a place to stay. We got to get to work an' settle down. No use a-lettin' the little fellas go hungry. That wasn't never Granma's way. She always et a good meal at a funeral."

The conserving lesson of the past is negated by the present economic reality. Ma's brave gesture fails as the family learns that California is a false goal. The imagery associated with California indicates these negations. Peter Lisca and Joseph Fontenrose have pointed to the major biblical parallels in *The Grapes of Wrath,* including those associating California and the Promised Land. The parallels are intensive, even more so than Lisca and Fontenrose suggest, and their function is ironic rather than associative. To begin with, California evokes images of plenty to eat and drink. The ironic fact is that California is the literal reverse of Canaan; there is little to eat and drink, at least for Okies; but California *is* the Promised Land so far as the family's experience there forces the full emergence of the group concept. Appropriately, the family enters California with a foreboding that runs counter to their expectations:

> Pa called, "We're here—we're in California!" They looked
> dully at the broken rock glaring under the sun, and across the
> river the terrible ramparts of Arizona.

They have crossed over, but the physical imagery foreshadows their actual human environment. The land is green across the river, but the biblical lists of landscape features are framed by the fact that they have been carrying Grandma's corpse. The human reality of Californian life is a living death, as the first camp, the Hooverville, suggests: "About the camp there hung a slovenly despair," everything is "grey" and "dirty," there is no work, no food, and no evident means of overcoming "despair." The deadly economic reality is explained by a young man in the Hooverville, when Tom asks why the police "shove along" the migrants:

> "Some say they don' want us to vote; keep us movin' so we
> can't vote. An' some says so we can't get on relief. An' some says
> if we set in one place we'd get organized."

That reply announces the political solution, the humanly possible way of countervailing power through organization. But the words are programmatic, not a revelation of character.

The difference in materials and in structure begins to appear at this point. The root of the matter is that Steinbeck is so compelled by the documentary facts that he permits their narration to take precedence over the central theme of the family's transformation into the group. And in moving the novel toward an affirmation of life in response to the facts, Steinbeck allows the Joads' experience in California to become a series of allegorical details within a panoramic structure. The narrowed scope of the materials and the schematic handling of the structure are visible in nearly every event in this part of the novel.

Casy's alternative to "despair," sacrificing himself for "the people," is almost wholly an allegorical solution. It is so abstractly schematic that at first none of the family understands its meaningful allegorical force—that loss of self leads to the group concept and thus to power to enforce the will of the group. Instead, the narrative is largely an account of the family's efforts to avoid starvation. The phrase "We got to eat" echoes through these concluding chapters. Ma's changing attitude toward hungry unknown children is ambiguous: "I dunno what to do. I can't rob the fambly. I got to feed the fambly." Ma grows more positive, later, when she is nagged by a storekeeper in the struck orchard:

> "Any reason you got to make fun? That help you any?" . . .
> "A fella got to eat," he began; and then, belligerantly, "A fella got a right to eat." "What fella?" Ma asked.

Ma asserts finally that only "the poor" constitute a group that practices charity:

> "I'm learnin' one thing good," she said. "Learnin' it all a time, ever' day. If you're in trouble or hurt or need—go to poor people. They're the only ones that'll help—the only ones."

"The poor" are identified with "the people," who, in turn are the emerging group. Their purity is allegorical, and, in its limitation, incredible. Steinbeck's handling of "the poor" in *In Dubious Battle* is much less schematic, and therefore far more credible. In general, romanticizing "the poor" is more successful in an outright fantasy like *Tortilla Flat* but Steinbeck commits himself to a measure of realism in *The Grapes of Wrath* that does not sort well with the allegorical division of "good" from "evil."

Romanticizing "the poor" extends beyond Ma's insight to an idealization of the "folk law" that Tom envisions as the fruit of his own experience in California—at a great distance from the "building" experience on the road:

> "I been thinkin' how it was in that gov'ment camp, how our folks took care a theirselves, an' if they was a fight they fixed it theirself; an' they wasn't no cops wagglin' their guns, but they was better order than them cops ever give. I been a-wonderin' why we can't do that all over. Throw out the cops

that ain't our people. All work together for our own thing—all
farm our own lan'.''

Presenting the reverse of Tom's beatific vision in an interchapter, Steinbeck
draws on the imagery of the novel's title:

> This vineyard will belong to the bank. Only the great owners
> can survive. . . . Men who can graft the trees and make the seed
> fertile and big can find no way to let the hungry people eat their
> produce. . . . In the souls of the people the grapes of wrath are
> filling and growing heavy, growing heavy for the vintage.

It is not vitally important that Steinbeck's prediction of some kind of
agrarian revolt has turned out to be wrong. The important artistic fact is
that "good," divided sharply, abstractly, from "evil," argues that Steinbeck is not interested in rendering the materials in any great depth.
Consider the contrast between the people in the government camp and in
the struck orchard. Point by point, the camp people are described as clean,
friendly, joyful, and organized, while in the struck orchard they are dirty,
suspicious, anxious, and disorganized by the police. Credibility gives way
to neat opposites, which are less than convincing because Steinbeck's
government camp is presented openly as a benevolent tyranny that aver-
ages out the will of "the people" to live in dignity and excludes people
unable or unwilling to accept that average.

Neat opposites can gather fictive conviction if they are realized through
individuals and in specific detail. There is something of that conviction in
specific action against specific men, as when the camp leaders exclude
troublemakers hired by business interests to break up the camp organization. There is more awkwardness in the exclusion of a small group of
religious fanatics obsessed with sin. An important factor is that these
people are genuinely Okies, not tools of the interests; another is that the
exclusion is necessary, not realistic, if the secular values of the group
concept are to prevail. Allowing for his selection and schematic treatment
of these materials, Steinbeck does engineer his manipulated point with
artistic skill. Fanaticism is considered a bad thing throughout the novel,
both as a religious stance and as a social phenomenon. Tom's first meeting
with Casy identifies "spirit" with emotional release, not a consciousness of
sin, and Casy announces his own discovery, made during his time in the
desert, of a social rather than an ethical connection between "spirit" and
sexual excitement. Further, fanaticism is identified repeatedly with a coer-
cive denial of life. Rose of Sharon is frightened, in the government camp,

by a fanatic woman's argument that dancing is sinful, that it means Rose will lose her baby. The woman's ignorance is placed against the secular knowledge of the camp manager:

> "I think the manager, he took [another girl who danced] away to drop her baby. He don' believe in sin. . . . Says the sin is bein' hungry. Says the sin is bein' cold."

She compounds ignorance by telling Ma that true religion demands fixed economic classes:

> "[A preacher] says 'They's wicketness in that camp.' He says, 'The poor is tryin' to be rich.' He says, 'They's dancin' an' huggin' when they should be wailin' an' moanin' in sin.' "

These social and economic denials of life are rooted in ignorance, not in spiritual enlightenment, and they are countered by the materialistic human-ism of the camp manager. So fanaticism is stripped of value and associated with business in its denial of life. The case is loaded further by the benevolent tyranny of the group. Fanatics are not punished for their opinions, or even for wrongdoing. They are merely excluded, or they exclude themselves.

A similar process is apparent in the group's control of social behavior, as when Ruthie behaves as a rugged individual in the course of a children's game:

> The children laid their mallets on the ground and trooped silently off the court. . . . Defiantly she hit the ball again. . . . She pretended to have a good time. And the children stood and watched. . . . For a moment she stared at them, and then she flung down the mallet and ran crying for home. The children walked back on the court. Pig-tails said to Winfield, "You can git in the nex' game." The watching lady warned them, "When she comes back an' wants to be decent, you let her. You was mean yourself, Amy."

The punishment is directive. The children are being trained to accept the group and to become willing parts of the group. The process is an expres-sion of "folk law" on a primary level. There is no doubt that Ruthie learned her correct place in the social body by invoking a suitably social punishment.

Perhaps the ugliness implicit in the tyranny of the group has become more visible lately. Certainly recent students of the phenomenon of mod-ern conformity could supply Steinbeck with very little essential insight.

The real trouble is precisely there. The tyranny of the group is visible in all of Steinbeck's instances (its ambiguity is most evident in Ruthie's case), which argues for Steinbeck's artistic honesty in rendering the materials. But he fails to see deeply enough, to see ugliness and ambiguity, because he has predetermined the absolute "good" of group behavior—an abstraction that precludes subtle technique and profound insight, on the order of Doc Burton's reservations concerning group-man. The result is a felt manipulation of values and a thinning of credibility.

Given this tendency, Steinbeck does not surprise us by dealing abstractly with the problem of leadership in the government camp. Since there is minimal narrative time in which to establish the moral purity of Jim Rawley, the camp manager, or of Ezra Huston, the chairman of the Central Committee, Steinbeck presents both men as allegorical figures. Particularly Jim Rawley. His introduction suggests his allegorical role. He is named only once, and thereafter he is called simply "the camp manager." His name is absorbed in his role as God. He is dressed "all in white," but he is not a remote God. "The frayed seams on his white coat" suggest his human availability, and his "warm" voice matches his social qualities. Nevertheless, there is no doubt that he is God visiting his charges:

> He put the cup on the box with the others, waved his hand, and walked down the line of tents. And Ma heard him speaking to the people as he went.

His identification with God is bulwarked when the fanatic woman calls him the devil:

> "She says you was the devil," [says Rose of Sharon]. "I know she does. That's because I won't let her make people miserable. . . . Don't you worry. She doesn't know."

What "she doesn't know" is everything the camp manager does know; and if he is not the devil, he must be God. But his very human, secular divinity—he can wish for an easier lot, and he is always tired from overwork—suggests the self-sacrifice that is Casy's function. The two men are outwardly similar. Both are clean and "lean as a picket," and the camp manager has "merry eyes" like Casy's when Tom meets Casy again. These resemblances would be trivial, except for a phrase that pulls them together and lends them considerable weight. Ezra Huston has no character to speak of, beyond his narrative function, except that when he has finished asking the men who try to begin a riot in the camp why they betrayed "their own people," he adds: "They don't know what they're doin'." This phrase foreshadows Casy's words to his murderer just before he is killed in an effort to break the strike: "You don't know what you're a-doin'." Just as these words associate Casy with Christ, so they associate the leaders in the government camp with Casy. Steinbeck's foreshortening indicates that, because Casy is established firmly as a "good" character, the leaders in the government camp must resemble Casy in that "good" identity.

The overall process is allegorical, permitting Steinbeck to assert that the camp manager and Ezra Huston are good men by definition and precluding the notion that leadership may be a corrupting role, as in *In Dubious Battle*. It follows that violence in the name of the group is "good," whereas it is "evil" in the name of business interests. The contrast is too neat, too sharp, to permit much final credibility in narrative or in characterization.

A still more extreme instance of Steinbeck's use of allegory is the process by which Tom Joad assumes the role of a leader. Tom's pastoral concept of the group is fully developed, and as the novel ends, Tom identifies himself through mystic insight with the group. Appropriately, Tom explains his insight to Ma because Tom's function is to act while Ma's function is to endure—in the name of the group. More closely, Ma's earlier phrase, "We're the people—we go on," is echoed directly in Tom's assurance when Ma fears for his life:

> "Well, maybe like Casy says, a fella ain't got a soul of his own, but on'y a piece of a big one—an' then——" "Then what, Tom?" "Then it don' matter. Then I'll be all aroun' in the dark. I'll be ever'where—wherever you look. . . . See? God, I'm talkin' like Casy. Comes of thinkin' about him so much. Seems like I can see him sometimes."

This anthropomorphic insight, borrowed from *To a God Unknown* and remotely from Emerson, is a serious idea, put seriously within the allegorical framework of the novel's close. Two structural difficulties result. First, Tom has learned more than Casy could have taught him—that identification *with* the group, rather than self-sacrifice *for* the group, is the truly effective way to kill the dehumanized "Bank." Here, it seems, the Christ/Casy, Saint Paul/Tom identifications were too interesting in themselves, for they limit Steinbeck's development of Tom's insight to a mechanical parallel, such as the suggestion that Tom's visions of Casy equate with Saint Paul's visions of Christ. Second, the connection between the good material life and Tom's mystical insight is missing. There is Steinbeck's close attention to

Tom's political education and to his revival of belief in a moral world. But, in the specific instance, the only bridge is Tom's sudden feeling that mystical insight connects somehow with the good material life. More precisely, the bridge is Steinbeck's own assertion, since Tom's mystical vision of pastoral bliss enters the narrative only as an abstract announcement on Steinbeck's part.

Characterization is, as might be assumed, affected by this abstracting tendency. Earlier, major characters such as Tom and Ma are "given" through actions in which they are involved, not through detached, abstract essays; increasingly, at the close, the method of presentation is the detached essay or the extended, abstract speech. Steinbeck's earlier, more realized presentation of Tom as a natural man measures the difference. Even a late event, Tom's instinctive killing of Casy's murderer, connects organically with Tom's previous "social" crimes—the murder in self-defense, for which Tom has finished serving a prison term when the novel begins, and the parole that Tom jumps to go with the family to California. In all of these crimes, Tom's lack of guilt or shame links with the idea that "the people" have a "natural" right to unused land—not to add life, liberty, and the pursuit of happiness—and that "the Bank" has nothing but an abstract, merely legal right to such land. Tom's mystical vision is something else; it is a narrative shock, not due to Tom's "natural" responses, but to the oversimplified type of the "good" man that Tom is made to represent in order to close the novel on a high and optimistic note. Tom is a rather complex man earlier on, and the thinning out of his character, in its absolute identification with the "good," is an inevitable result of allegorizing.

Style suffers also from these pressures. Tom's speech has been condemned, as Emerson's writing never is, for mawkishness, for maudlin lushness, for the soft, rotten blur of intellectual evasion. Style is a concomitant of structure; its decline is an effect, not a cause. Tom's thinking is embarrassing, not as thought, but as the stylistic measure of a process of manipulation that is necessary to close the novel on Steinbeck's terms.

The final scene, in which Rose of Sharon breastfeeds a sick man, has been regarded universally as the nadir of bad Steinbeck, yet the scene is no more and no less allegorical than earlier scenes in this final part. Purely in a formal sense, it parallels Tom's mystical union or identification with the group: It affirms that "life" has become more important than "family" in a specific action, and, as such, it denotes the emergence of the group concept. In that light, the scene is a technical accomplishment. Yet it is a disaster from the outset, not simply because it is sentimental; its execution, through the leading assumption, is incredible. Rose of Sharon is supposed to become Ma's alter ego by taking on her burden of moral insight, which, in turn, is similar to the insight that Tom reaches. There is no preparation for Rose of Sharon's transformation and no literary justification except a merely formal symmetry that makes it desirable, in spite of credibility, to devise a repetition. Tom, like Ma, undergoes a long process of education; Rose of Sharon is characterized in detail throughout the novel as a protected, rather thoughtless, whining girl. Possibly her miscarriage produces an unmentioned, certainly mystical change in character. More likely the reader will notice the hand of the author, forcing Rose of Sharon into an unprepared and purely formalistic role.

Once given this degree of manipulation, direct sentimentality is no surprise. Worse, the imagistic shift from anger to sweetness, from the grapes of wrath to the milk of human kindness, allows the metaphor to be uplifted, but at the cost of its structural integrity. The novel is made to close with a forced image of optimism and brotherhood, with an audacious upbeat that cries out in the wilderness. I have no wish to deny the value or the real power of good men, optimism, or brotherhood. The point is that Steinbeck imposes an unsupported conclusion upon materials which themselves are thinned out and manipulated. The increasingly grotesque episodes (and their leading metaphors) prove that even thin and manipulated materials resist the conclusion that is drawn from them, for art visits that revenge on its mistaken practitioners.

To argue that no better conclusion was available at the time, granting the country's social and political immaturity and its economic innocence, simply switches the issue from art to politics. No artist is obliged to provide solutions to the problems of the socio-politico-economic order, however "engaged" his work may be. Flaubert did not present a socioeducational program to help other young women to avoid Emma Bovary's fate. The business of the artist is to present a situation. If he manipulates the materials or forces them to conclusions that violate credibility—especially if he has a visible design upon us—his work will thin, the full range of human possibility will not be available to him, and to that extent he will have failed as an artist.

We must not exclude the likelihood, not that Steinbeck had no other conclusion at hand, but that his predisposition was to see a resolution in the various allegorical and panoramic arrangements that close out *The Grapes of Wrath;* Steinbeck's earlier work argues for that likelihood.

Yet that is not all there is to John Steinbeck. If he becomes the willing victim of abstract, horrendously schematic manipulations as *The Grapes of Wrath* nears its close still he is capable of better things. He demonstrates these potentialities particularly in minor scenes dealing with minor characters, so the negative force of the imposed conclusion is lessened.

Consider the scene in which Ruthie and Winfield make their way (along with the family) from the flooded boxcar to the barn where Rose of Sharon will feed the sick man. The intention of the scene is programmatic: the children's identification with the group concept. The overt content is the essentially undamaged survival of their sense of fun and of beauty. Significantly, the action makes no directly allegorical claim on the reader, unlike the rest of the concluding scenes.

Ruthie finds a flower along the road, "a scraggly geranium gone wild, and there was one rain-beaten blossom on it." The common flower, visualized, does not insist on the identity of the beaten but surviving beauty in pure nature with the uprooted, starved children of all the migrants. The scene is developed implicitly, in dramatic, imagistic terms. Ruthie and Winfield struggle to possess the petals for playthings, and Ma forces Ruthie to be kind:

> Winfield held his nose near to her. She wet a petal with her tongue and jabbed it cruelly on his nose. "You little son-of-a-bitch," she said softly. Winfield felt for the petal with his fingers, and pressed it down on his nose. They walked quickly after the others. Ruthie felt how the fun was gone. "Here," she said. "Here's some more. Stick some on your forehead."

The scene recapitulates the earlier scene on the playground of the government camp. Here, as there, Winfield is the innocent, and Ruthie's cruelty is changed by external pressure (the other children, Ma's threat) to an official kindness that transcends itself to become a genuine kindness when "the fun was gone." The observed basis of the present scene is the strained relationship that usually exists between an older sister and a younger brother. There is no visible effort to make the scene "fit" a predetermined allegorical scheme. Ruthie's kind gesture leads into Rose of Sharon's, as child to adult, and both scenes project the affirmative values—the survival of optimism, brotherhood, kindliness, goodness—that are the substance of the group concept at the conclusion. The children's quarrel and reconciliation is a relatively unloaded action, an event in itself. Tom's affirmation is nondramatic, a long, deeply mystical speech to Ma. Rose of Sharon's affirmation is out of character and frankly incredible. Uncle John's symbolic action derives from his own guilt but expresses a universal anger.

As the scene between the children is exceptional, Steinbeck's development of the flood scene is typical. Allegorical intentions override narrative power: The family's struggle against the flood is intended to equate with its surviving will to struggle against hopelessness; Pa, Uncle John, and Al are exhausted but not beaten. Tom's insight precedes the flood; Rose of Sharon's agreement to breastfeed the sick man follows it. In the larger frame, neither extreme of drouth or flood can exhaust the will and the vitality of the people. The dense texture of these panoramic materials is impressive. They lie side by side, at different levels of the "willing suspension of disbelief," depending on whether they are convincing narrative actions or palpable links in an arranged allegory. Hence, there is no great sense of a concluding "knot," an organic fusion of parts; there is no more than a formulated ending, a pseudoclose that does not convince because its design is an a priori assertion of structure, not the supportive and necessary skeleton of a realized context. Here structure and materials fail to achieve a harmonious relationship.

These final scenes are not hackwork. We cannot apply to Steinbeck, even here, the slurring remark that F. Scott Fitzgerald aimed at Thomas Wolfe: "The stuff about the GREAT VITAL HEART OF AMERICA is just simply corny." Steinbeck's carefully interwoven strands of character, metaphor, and narrative argue a conscious, skillful intention, not a sudden lapse of material or of novelistic ability. Even in failure, Steinbeck is a formidable technician. His corn, here, if it exists, is not a signal of failed ability.

Steinbeck's feeling that *The Grapes of Wrath* must close on an intense level of sweetness, of optimism and affirmation, is not seriously in doubt. His ability to use the techniques of structure to this end is evident. The earlier novels demonstrate his able willingness to skillfully apply an external structure, to mold, or at least to mystify, somewhat recalcitrant materials. The letter withdrawing *L'Affaire Lettuceburg* suggests that Steinbeck is aware of having that willing skill—"just twisting this people out of shape"—and of having to resist its lures in this most serious work. So for the critic there is a certain horrid fascination in Steinbeck's consistent, enormously talented demonstration of aesthetic failure in the last quarter of *The Grapes of Wrath*.

The failure is not a matter of "sprawling asides and extravagances," or the more extreme motivational simplicities of naturalism, or a lapse in the remarkably sustained folk idiom and the representative epic scope. The failure lies in the means Steinbeck utilizes to achieve the end.

The first three quarters of the novel are masterful. Characters are presented through action; symbolism intensifies character and action; the

central theme of transformation from self to group develops persuasively
in a solid, realized documentary context. The final quarter of the novel
presents a difference in every respect. Characters are fitted or forced into
allegorical roles, heightened beyond the limits of credibility, to the point
that they thin out or become frankly unbelievable. Scenes are developed
almost solely as links in an allegorical pattern. Texture is reduced to
documentation, and allegorical signs replace symbolism. The result is a
hollowed rhetoric, a manipulated affirmation, a soft twist of insistent
sentiment. These qualities deny the conceptual theme by simplifying it, by
reducing the facts of human and social complexity to simple opposites.

The reduction is not inherent in the materials, which are rendered
magnificently in earlier parts of the novel. The reduction is the consequence of a structural choice—to apply allegory to character, metaphor,
and theme. In short, *The Grapes of Wrath* could conceivably have a
sweetly positive conclusion without an absolute, unrestrained dependence
on allegory. Yet the least subtle variety of that highly visible structural
technique, with its objectionably simplified, manipulative ordering of materials, is precisely the element that prevails in the final part of *The Grapes
of Wrath*.

Why? Steinbeck is aware of various technical options, and he is able
to make use of them earlier in the novel. As we have seen in the previous
novels, with the exception of *In Dubious Battle,* Steinbeck draws on
allegory to stiffen or to heighten fictions that are too loose—too
panoramic—to achieve the semblance of a dramatic structure purely by
means of technique. Apparently Steinbeck was not offended aesthetically
by the overwhelming artificiality that results from an extreme dependence
on allegory. That the contemporary naturalistic or symbolic novel requires
a less simple or rigid structure clearly escapes Steinbeck's attention.

On the contrary, Steinbeck is greatly attracted to some extreme kind
of external control in much of the immediately preceding work and in
much of the succeeding work. During the rest of his career, Steinbeck does
not attempt seriously, on the massive scale of *The Grapes of Wrath,* to
achieve a harmonious relationship between structure and materials. He
prefers some version of the control that flaws the last quarter of *The
Grapes of Wrath*.

This judgment offers a certain reasonableness in the otherwise wild
shift from *The Grapes of Wrath* to the play-novelettes.

WARREN FRENCH

John Steinbeck: A Usable Concept
of Naturalism

The fundamental question in any study of "literary naturalism" is the utility of the term itself. Let us begin with the definition provided by the *Oxford Companion to American Literature* as representative of "received opinion":

> Naturalism, critical term applied to the method of literary composition that aims at a detached, scientific objectivity in the treatment of natural man. It is thus more inclusive and less selective than realism ... and holds to the philosophy of determinism. It conceives of man as controlled by his passions, or by his social and economic environment and circumstances. Since in this view man has no free will, the naturalistic writer does not attempt to make moral judgments, and as a determinist he leans toward pessimism.

There is more concerning the origins of the term, but enough is quoted to indicate that the problem is whether such a definition actually applies to any literary works.

Edwin H. Cady thinks not. In *The Light of Common Day: Realism in American Fiction,* he explains his concept of the "naturalistic" position:

> The universe was reduced to a blind flow of mindless, dicey forces. Man was reduced to the merest organism fighting meaninglessly, at the mercy of chance and force, to foredoomed loss.

From *American Literary Naturalism: A Reassessment,* edited by Yoshinobu Hakutani and Lewis Fried. © 1975 by Warren French. Carl Winter Universitäts Verlag, 1975.

The naturalist's "sense of reality," Cady finds,

> stemmed from the imagination of a tough-mindedly ultimate,
> hard Darwinism. But it became a vision still further reduced by
> post-Darwinian science and scientism. . . . The new knowledge
> led not to more but less certainty, not control but mystery and
> defeat as the dimensions and processes of the world pushed
> past the limits of imagination. Even before Einstein, the possi-
> bilities of understanding, of getting an education, in human
> terms vanished into mist.

Cady conceives of the naturalist's position being that man cannot
possibly intellectually or imaginatively control his environment—a position that leads him to observe that "there really are no naturalists in
American literature." He is not aware, he maintains, "of a work of fiction
which will stand adequately and consistently for the naturalistic sensibility."

His conclusion is shared—though couched in gentler terms—by Lillian
R. Furst, who has contributed "Naturalism" to a series of pamphlets on
"The Critical Idiom." She reaches the conclusion that "fortunately, with
rare exceptions, the adherents of Naturalism did not quite practice what
they preached, largely, one suspects, because it proved totally impractica-
ble." "The paradoxical conclusion emerges," she goes on,

> that Naturalism succeeded best where it seemed to fail, i.e.
> where it departed from rather than outstripped its own inten-
> tions. As a serious attempt to bring the arts into line with the
> sciences it failed, as it was bound to do in so misguided an
> undertaking.

Thus recent theorists conclude that the term *naturalism* as convention-
ally employed in literary criticism does not actually apply to any creative
works. Both Cady and Furst are uncertain that literature can indeed
achieve "detached, scientific objectivity" and avoid "moral judgments." I
share their doubts because it seems to me that what distinguishes *literature*
from *kitsch*, even more than style and originality, is passion; and passion is
incompatible with scientific objectivity and moral neutrality.

Even Charles Child Walcutt is compelled to concede that the term
naturalism as standardly used in literary discussion doesn't really apply to
any creative works, because "a work that was perfectly controlled by
theory of materialistic determinism would not be a novel but a report."
"The formal looseness of so much contemporary fiction," he adds, "would
seem to indicate that naturalism cannot achieve the coherence and integ-

rity that go with a completely acceptable criticism of life" (*American Literary Naturalism: A Divided Stream*).

Walcutt attempts to salvage the term by arguing that "it is irrelevant to ask whether" a novel like Dreiser's *An American Tragedy* is optimistic or pessimistic, "the question is whether it is true." But truth provides criteria for evaluating reports, not fictions. (Fiction may contain a kind of truth, but it need not be factually verifiable.) He also argues that free will and ethical responsibility are not really "absent from the naturalistic novel," but are "rather, taken away from the protagonist and the other characters and transferred to the reader and to society at large."

But all novels may be discussed in terms of either characters or readers, and a term that is useful only for discussing novels as they affect readers could be employed only in discussions of readers' experiences. It would be of no use in distinguishing characters in one kind of novel from those in another. Walcutt perceives a quality that does distinguish "naturalistic novels" from others, but he fails to come up with a method of using the term in making any general classification of novels on the basis of the characters portrayed. As Cady argues, for a term "to have any viable critical use," it must "distinguish some kind of true, of successful literature from other kinds." Since *naturalism* seems to fit only theoretical examples of a misguided theory, perhaps the time has come to dismiss it from the critical vocabulary.

Working inductively from actual novels rather than deductively from philosophical premises, however, Donald Pizer proposes that the term might be usefully preserved not to describe nonexistent illustrations of an a priori position, but rather to provide a useful label for certain successful works of literature that deal with characters demonstrably different from those in other successful works—in the great bulk, in fact, of those successful novels produced in the first century after Samuel Richardson's *Pamela*.

In "Late Nineteenth-Century Naturalism," Pizer advances "a modified definition" that must be quoted at length as a springboard for any useful future discussion of "literary naturalism":

> I suggest that the naturalistic novel usually contains two tensions or contradictions, and that the two in conjunction comprise both an interpretation of experience and a particular aesthetic recreation of experience. In other words, the two constitute the theme and form of the naturalistic novel. The first tension is that between subject matter of the naturalistic novel and the concept of man which emerges from this subject

matter. The naturalist populates his novel primarily from the lower middle class or lower class. His characters are the poor, the uneducated, the unsophisticated. . . . The second tension involves the theme of the naturalistic novel. The naturalist often describes his characters as though they are conditioned and controlled by environment, heredity, instinct or chance. But he also suggests a compensating humanistic value in his characters or their fates which affirms the significance of the individual and of his life. The tension here is that between the naturalist's desire to represent in fiction the new, discomforting truths which he found in the ideas and life of his late nineteenth-century world, and also his desire to find some meaning in experience which reasserts the validity of the human enterprise. . . .

The naturalistic novel is therefore not so superficial or reductive as it implicity appears to be in its conventional definition. . . . It suggests that even the least significant human being can feel and strive powerfully and can suffer the extraordinary consequences of his emotions.

(Realism and Naturalism in Nineteenth-Century
American Literature)

Long as this quotation runs, some important points about the products of this enterprise have been omitted because I have no reservations about them. I am not entirely satisfied, however, with the key passages quoted. What bothers me about this well conceived and generally persuasive theory are Pizer's stipulation that the naturalistic novel deals primarily with the lower social orders and his use of the term "least significant human being" because such emphasis risks equating the "naturalistic novel" with what is usually called "the proletarian novel." The problem about those "conditioned" characters that Pizer speaks of is not that they lack "significance"—their actions may have calamitous importance—but that, as Walcutt recognizes, they lack control over the consequences of their behavior. (Such characters may, of course, console themselves by calling their lack of self-discipline a lack of "significance," especially to shift responsibilities for their failures from themselves to a hostile world.)

The important way in which Pizer answers Cady's objections is by acknowledging that even those who do lack such control "can feel and strive powerfully," as well as suffer (and certainly make others suffer). Pizer does not seem to me, however, to stress sufficiently that the characters he speaks of are conceived by their creators as "feeling" rather than "thinking." They are created like the young lovers in Frank Norris's *Blix* as having brains "almost as empty of thought or reflection as those of two fine, clean animals." Such characters surely can—like this pair—"feel and strive powerfully," but their irresponsibility bodes well for no one.

Novels focused on such characters need to be distinguished from those that deal primarily with characters seeking to exercise disciplined control over situations. Curiously, previous discussions of literary naturalism have not settled on a descriptive term for such "non-naturalistic" works. This term itself has undesirable supernatural or fantastic connotations; but this gap in the critical vocabulary is easily remedied by appropriating a term suggested by Henry James in his preface to the 1907 edition of *Roderick Hudson*—"the drama of consciousness." That James himself was keenly aware of the distinction between the two kinds of creative intentions that I wish to contrast here—and even felt in some measure Cady's later annoyance about the "naturalistic" viewpoint—is evident from his statement in an essay on the novelist, Mrs. Humphry Ward (1892):

> Life, for Mrs. Humphry Ward, as the subject of a large canvas, means predominantly the life of the thinking, the life of the sentient creature, whose chronicler at the present hour, so little is he in fashion, it has been almost an originality on her part to become.

The striking distinction between the characters that Dreiser creates for *Sister Carrie* and that James creates for *Roderick Hudson* is that the former are not represented as being conscious of what they are doing or capable of any self-analysis of their motivations; whereas the latter are almost obsessively preoccupied with self-conscious analysis. As Alan Rose astutely points out, Dreiser's heroine's view of experience is "as immature at the end of *Sister Carrie,* when she has wealth, as it was at the beginning." A useful distinction may thus be made between fictions that deal essentially with characters presented by their creators as aware of what they are doing and of the potential consequences of these actions and fictions that deal essentially with characters envisioned by their creators as altogether at the mercy of such forces as "environment, heredity, instinct and chance."

Occasionally the paths of the two kinds of characters cross, as in Henry James's "The Real Thing," but James's interest is in the consciousness of the artist, not the economic salvation of the Monarchs. This illustration demonstrates, however, that while "naturalistic" characters are likely to come from the lower orders, they are not found only there. There are poor and humble people who know what they are doing—who sometimes even choose poverty over contaminated wealth like Faulkner's Ike McCaslin; and there are characters with money (though often not for long) who literally do not know what they are doing, like Fitzgerald's Buchanans or Faulkner's Compsons. John Steinbeck captures in a conversation in *Cannery Row* the difference between the rich and powerful driven by blind ambition and those who are poor by choice not chance. Two men the world would call wastrels discuss a friend:

> Hazel kicked sand on the fire. "I bet Mack could of been president of the U.S. if he wanted," he said.
> "What could he do with it if he had it?" Jones asked. "There wouldn't be no fun in that."

The distinction that I seek to make can be most precisely established, however, by analysis of one of the last passages in *The Red Badge of Courage*—a passage that suggests why Crane's work after *Maggie* and *George's Mother* had posed great problems for those who have attempted to associate him with naturalism. Crane observes that Henry Fleming smiled:

> For he saw that the world was a world made for him, though many discovered it to be made of oaths and walking sticks. He had rid himself of the red sickness of battle. . . . He had been an animal blistered and sweating in the heat and pain of war. He turned now with a lover's thirst to images of tranquil skies, fresh meadows, cool brooks—an existence of soft and eternal peace.

The characters in "naturalistic" novels are precisely those, like Crane's Maggie, who discover the world to be made of "oaths and walking sticks" and who are at last overwhelmed by it because they cannot exercise any control over their fates (even Jim Conklin in *Red Badge* belongs in this group, but the novel is Henry's story, not Jim's), while in the word "lover" Crane provides precisely the term to describe the other kind of self-conscious characters that I have been discussing. "Lovers" of course, not necessarily in the physically passionate sense but in Crane's sense of those who love life and its promises.

Crane's distinction serves to clear up a passage in the opening pages of *Sister Carrie* that I have found troubling. Doting upon his mindlessly happy creation, Dreiser observes that "Self-interest with her was high, but not strong. It was, nevertheless, her guiding characteristic." What distinction can Dreiser have had in mind when he contrasts adjectives that are usually synonymous as descriptions of states of mind unless he wishes to suggest that Carrie has an overwhelming ("high" in the sense of a natural phenomenon like temperature, not under the control of the individual) animalistic instinct for self-preservation, but not a self-conscious ("strong" in the sense of developed and disciplined by deliberate training) awareness of how to advance her own interests? Such an explanation accounts better than any fears of censure on Dreiser's part for Carrie's entirely passive contribution to her success in attracting Drouet, then Hurstwood, and finally the theatrical director who starts her on the road to stardom. This concept of Carrie also suggests how Dreiser can speak in the final paragraph of the novel of the "blind strivings" of the human heart and argue that Carrie may "dream" such happiness as she may never "feel." The naturalistic character lives in a dream-world of intense but vaguely formulated desires. He may strive powerfully, as Pizer suggests, but he strives aimlessly.

Few of these characters are so lucky as Carrie; most authors feel that they are going to find the world made of "oaths and walking sticks," as ultimately Hurstwood does. The lover who finds the world made for him usually does so because he can advance on his own initiative—as Thoreau prescribes in *Walden*—"confidently in the direction of his dreams," understanding both the visionary quality of the dreams and the necessity for disciplined action to make them come true. Carrie makes out as well as she does, because she is not a real person in an unfeeling world, but the fictional creation of an infatuated artist.

II

Applied to John Steinbeck's fiction, the contrasts that I have suggested between the "naturalistic novel" and the "drama of consciousness" provide a firm basis for perceiving three distinct periods in the novelist's career and even suggest reasons for his rise to eminence during the 1930s and his much-discussed decline as an artist after World War II.

Previous discussions of Steinbeck's "naturalism" have not provided a basis for such discriminations. Charles Child Walcutt discusses Steinbeck at length in *American Literary Naturalism: A Divided Stream*, but apparently finds the characters and the point of view from which they are shaped unchanging, as he notes "in novel after novel a belief in science, a firm belief in material causation." While this observation is sound enough, it provided no basis for distinguishing any stages in Steinbeck's artistic development, as I believe that the distinction I have been drawing on the basis of the type of characters emphasized in certain novels does.

Steinbeck's first two novels—*Cup of Gold* (1929) and *To a God Unknown* (1933—published after *The Pastures of Heaven,* but conceived earlier)—are definitely not "naturalistic" as I propose we use the term. Henry Morgan (the pirate in the first novel) and Joseph Wayne (hero of the second) both consciously choose the courses that they follow—the former to self-aggrandizement and the latter to the potential salvation of the community—and they accept the consequences of their choices. Morgan realizes that a man must "split up" before civilization; Joseph Wayne chooses self-sacrifice to restore the fertility of the land.

Both the ruthless exploiter Morgan and the self-sacrificing Wayne, however, illustrate that during the "waste land" years of the 1920s, Steinbeck did not believe that realizing one's dreams could be reconciled with achieving personal security—a view shared by most of the "lost generation" writers— Fitzgerald, Hemingway, Sinclair Lewis, especially Ring Lardner. Conscious control of one's behavior is purchased in both *Cup of Gold* and *To a God Unknown* at a frightening price. Like the other writers, Steinbeck seems to have felt early in his career that too much self-consciousness can be dehumanizing. If thoughtlessness produces chaos, too much thought produces the robotized world of Elmer Rice's play *The Adding Machine* or Fritz Lang's film *Metropolis. To a God Unknown* implies that the price of too much knowledge and control must be expiatory death; *Cup of Gold* cynically suggests that one survives by giving up one's dreams.

With *The Pastures of Heaven,* Steinbeck abandons altogether these speculations and switches his attention to those who literally do not know what they are doing. His next five novels or novelettes—as well as the short stories written during the same years between 1931 and 1938—are all "naturalistic" as I have defined the term and form a distinctive body among his work of some of his most successful writings.

The Pastures of Heaven is a heavily ironic collection of ten stories of life in a deceptively beautiful valley, framed by a prologue and epilogue. That the name of "The Pastures of Heaven" is ironic is stressed by the prologue that explains that the valley was named for the impression that its unspoiled beauty made around 1776 on a Spanish corporal who was returning to captivity some Indians who had abandoned Christianity and hard labor for a carefree, pagan life. The corporal's dream of spending his last days contentedly in this valley vanishes when he wastes away with a venereal disease presented him, ironically, by an Indian woman. The defeat of his dream establishes the pattern for the tales constituting the book, which becomes—through the presence of the Munroe family—a novel rather than simply a collection of related tales.

The Munroes provide the link between the stories. The basic pattern followed in all of them is foreshadowed in a conversation between Bert Munroe and T. B. Allen, the valley storekeeper, at the end of the second chapter, which relates the misfortunes that have in the past befallen both the Munroes and the farm that they have bought in the valley:

> Bert had been frowning soberly as a new thought began to work in his mind. "I've had a lot of bad luck," he said. "I've been in a lot of businesses and every one turned out bad. When I came down here, I had a kind of idea that I was under a curse. . . . And what do I do? First thing out of the box, I buy a place that's supposed to be under a curse. Well, I just happened to think, maybe my curse and the farm's curse got to fighting and killed each other off. I'm dead certain they've gone anyway."
>
>   The men laughed with him. T. B. Allen whacked his hand down on the counter. "That's a good one," he cried. "But here's a better one. Maybe your curse and the farm's curse has mated and gone into a gopher hole like a pair of rattlesnakes. Maybe there'll be a lot of baby curses crawling around the Pastures the first thing we know."

Allen's is the better prediction. Though Munroe's personal fortunes flourish after buying the farm that has been a curse to others, out of the union of his curse with the farm's comes a brood of curses for other residents of the valley. The Munroes are never really responsible in any conscious sense for the tragedies they precipitate; they are always well-meaning. Their curse, it soon becomes evident, is that they never know the right thing to say or do, so that they have the calamitous effect of upsetting the precariously maintained equilibrium of insecure people. Too thoughtless to recognize their propensity for saying and doing the wrong thing, the Munroes constantly push themselves into positions that enable them to wreak havoc in the lives of others. "Thoughtless," in several senses, is the key word here. Because the Munroes never bother to find out the truth, they are continually at the mercy of their own erroneous preconceptions. They do strive powerfully, but always banefully, destroying not just the happiness of their neighbors, but even the mind and health of their younger son.

Steinbeck carefully avoids in *The Pastures of Heaven*, however, the question of whether the Munroes could have behaved differently. He does not suggest whether their thoughtlessness is congenital or learned; he is interested in this early novel only in the strikingly ironic contrast between expectations and fulfillments, symbolized by the contrast between the natural beauty of the Pastures of Heaven and the unbeautiful lives of its inhabitants.

Although Steinbeck often insisted during the 1930s especially that he was interested in the "how" rather than the "why" of things, only *The Pastures of Heaven* and some of the short stories in *The Long Valley,* like "Flight" and "The Snake," simply present naturalistic ironies. In the other novels of the period Steinbeck seeks out the sources of the troubles that beset "natural man."

Although not published as a unit until the appearance of *The Long Valley* in 1938, *The Red Pony* should probably be regarded as Steinbeck's next extended work, for parts of it began to appear in magazines before the publication of *Tortilla Flat.*

The Red Pony is a rare kind of work—a successful naturalistic comedy. As already observed, naturalistic characters are likely to find life made of "oaths and walking sticks." Writers about naturalistic characters tend to be pessimistic because they can't believe that things can work out well if the characters cannot discipline themselves and exercise some control over the world around them. Probably naturalistic comedies can be written only about children and child-like people, who succeed in finding someone to take care of them (as Dreiser takes care of Carrie). Even children (like Tularecito in *The Pastures of Heaven*) and child-like people who have found a guardian (like Lennie in *Of Mice and Men*) come to tragic ends in Steinbeck's work. *The Red Pony* deals actually with the development of a consciousness; but it remains a naturalistic work because it carries young Jody Tiflin just to that point where he exhibits a sense of self-conscious responsibility through a symbolic gesture. It does not press on to a point at which Jody becomes capable of conscious mature action as Casy and Tom Joad will be in *The Grapes of Wrath.* Perhaps Steinbeck's very point is that the only possible naturalistic comedy presents the action that paves the way for a future drama of consciousness.

While each of the four parts of *The Red Pony* may be read separately, together they tell a unified story of a boy's growth from selfish ignorance to compassionate enlightenment as his own experiences teach him to see the world, not as he wishes it to be, but as it is. Through the four stories, Jody Tiflin learns from four personal experiences of the fallibility of man (which leads to the death of his pony in "The Gift"), the wearing out of man (through the story of the old man who goes to die in "The Great Mountains"), the unreliability of nature (through the death of the mare in giving birth to a colt in "The Promise"), and finally the exhaustibility of nature itself, which leaves "a line of old men along the shore hating the ocean because it stopped them" after the taming of the frontier described in "The Leader of the People."

One might expect to find *The Red Pony* followed by the history of a grown-up Jody using his hard-bought wisdom to make the world a more tolerable place. But Steinbeck was not ready to create this character. His next books are pessimistic tales of defeat.

Perhaps the most flawless piece of "naturalism" that Steinbeck produced is the short story, "Flight." Nineteen-year-old Pepé, oldest child of a poor widow, is a lazy and not very bright boy, who spends most of his time practicing flicking the knife he has inherited from his father. When his mother is at last forced to send him to town alone, he kills a man who called him names that—as a man—he cannot allow. He is obliged to flee into the mountains, where his horse is shot from under him and he loses his rifle. A stone cut between his fingers begins to infect his whole arm. He reaches the peak of the ridge, but he has been followed. Cut down by a bullet, his falling body starts a little avalanche that buries his head.

Like Dreiser's Clyde Griffiths in *An American Tragedy,* Pepé is a cocky and impetuous but mentally limited young man who is destroyed when a social situation places upon him responsibilities that he is unequipped to assume. *Tortilla Flat, In Dubious Battle,* and *Of Mice and Men* are fundamentally expanded variations on the story of Pepé.

It may be difficult to think of *Tortilla Flat* as naturalistic because of the stylized and somewhat condescending good humor with which Steinbeck approaches his "paisano" characters. Writers like Frank Norris and Dreiser have led us to expect "naturalistic" fiction to be pontifical and humorless. Even such arch-foes of the "genteel tradition" shared its squeamish scruple that it's unseemly to be frivolous about human misery and degradation. Yet *Tortilla Flat* does finally share—despite its carnival atmosphere—the pessimism characteristic of naturalistic writing. However joyfully the paisanos swagger toward their ends, these ends are not happy. The story of Danny is actually an extended illustration of Henry Morgan's observation in *Cup of Gold* that "civilization will split up a character, and he who refuses to split goes under." Danny is a kind of legendary wild man—the kind of unrestrained individual that many oppressed by the pressures of civilization think that they would like to be.

But when Danny inherits two houses from his grandfather, he begins to succumb to the temptations of civilization. As he settles down, however, he begins "to feel the beating of time" that he had never been conscious of before. He sees how "every day was the same" with his friends; and he begins to long for the "good old days" when "the weight of property was not upon him." His friends try to help, but "it was not coddling Danny wanted, it was freedom." He surrenders to his longing, and disappears into the woods; but he has not fled soon enough. Now he finds the old wild life difficult and exhausting. He returns home beaten and apathetic.

To restore his spirits, his friends stage a huge party. At the height of the revelry, Danny challenges all present; and when none will fight, he shouts, "Then I will go out to The One who can fight. I will find the Enemy who is worthy of Danny!" He stalks out. Then his friends

> heard his roaring challenge. . . . And then, behind the house, in the gulch, they heard an answering challenge so fearful and so chill that their spines wilted like nasturtium stems under frost. . . . They heard Danny charge to the fray. They heard his last shrill cry of defiance, and then a thump. And then silence.

Steinbeck never identifies the "Enemy." Each reader may interpret the term for himself as referring to God, fate, some cycle of nature, or whatever he envisions as imposing limits on man and obliging him to conform to some system rather than live a law unto himself. Steinbeck does not editorialize about the force that drives Danny to his death, but he gives a clue to his concept of it by having Danny observe of another man, a dog-catcher, "It is not so easy to catch dogs when it is your business to catch dogs." It is easy to dream of freedom, but not to remain a free agent. Danny does not have the resources that would enable him either to adjust to a civilized life or to revert to his old, wild one; he cannot achieve the consciousness that would enable him to transcend the natural condition that dooms him.

The leading characters of *In Dubious Battle* are, like paisanos, social outsiders, though not even so sharp-witted. What differentiates Mac and Jim, two "red" labor organizers, from Steinbeck's earlier characters is their dedication to a "cause." They are spurred into action by their commitment to a vision of life, so that they are not, like Danny, victims of an unidentifiable force that intervenes between them and the achievement of a perfect harmony with life, but rather of a particular program to which they commit themselves without fully grasping the implications of such commitment. They differ (like George in *Of Mice and Men*) from the Munroes and Danny in being moved by a vision that transcends their own selfish ego; Steinbeck is beginning to move painfully—and not very hopefully— toward the selfless vision of *The Grapes of Wrath*.

"We've a job to do," Mac tells Doc Burton in *In Dubious Battle*. "We've got no time to mess around with high-falutin' ideas." "Yes,"

Burton replies, "and so you start your work not knowing your medium. And your ignorance trips you up every time."

No exchange could better sum up the situation of the characters I describe as "naturalistic." Although this most pessimistic of Steinbeck's works portrays a strike in the Torgas Valley apple orchards of California, it focuses upon the brief career as a Communist activist of Jim Nolan. Sent out to assist a veteran organizer, he discovers at last a meaning in life; but tricked by vigilantes seeking to break the strike, he is lured to his death in an ambush.

Doc Burton tells the surviving partner:

> "You practical men always lead practical men with stomachs. And something always gets out of hand. Your men get out of hand, they don't follow the rules of common sense, and you practical men either deny that it is so, or refuse to think about it. And when someone wonders what it is that makes a man with a stomach something more than your rule allows, why you howl, 'Dreamer, mystic, metaphysician!' ... In all history there are no men who have come to such wild-eyed confusion and bewilderment as practical men leading men with stomachs."

Burton, of course, is striving for as complete self-consciousness as possible; and if he were to prevail, the novel might have turned into a drama of consciousness offering the final flickering of hope that *The Grapes of Wrath* does. But in this most pessimistic of Steinbeck's novels, the consciously thoughtful man is doomed as surely as those who are incapable of examining their commitments. On his way to visit a wounded man one night, the doctor simply disappears. There is no survival even for the man of good will in the "naturalistic" world of oaths and walking sticks.

George survives in *Of Mice and Men,* but his dream has been shattered. As in many of the short stories collected in *The Long Valley,* a woman precipitates the tragic dénouement; but the girl herself is as much victim as her victims. The real villain is her insensitive husband, although he, too, cannot really be held responsible, because he is scarcely more intelligent than the hulking innocent who becomes his prey. The whole story is simply of "something that happened" (as Steinbeck first titled the work)—the world just hasn't been made right, so that dreams are the only things that can keep men going.

Two itinerant ranch-hands, George and Lennie, have joined forces and share a dream of some day owning a little place of their own. Although George maintains that Lennie "ain't no cuckoo," he is undeniably overdeveloped physically and underdeveloped mentally—a powerful giant with an infant's brain who accidentally kills the rabbits and puppies he likes to fondle. George has promised Lennie's aunt to look out for the giant. Although George complains that the arrangement cramps his style, he derives from it the benefit of having someone to take care of and share a dream with.

The hopelessness of the dream is suggested by an early revelation that the pair has had to run away from their last job because of Lennie's supposedly molesting a girl. George senses trouble at the new location as soon as he meets Curley, the boss's son, and his flirtatious wife. On Sunday afternoon while the other hands are absorbed by a horseshoe tournament, the girl gets Lennie to feel her soft hair. When he begins to muss it, she panics, and he breaks her neck. When George discovers what has happened, he realizes that the dream is over. In a grove where they had agreed to meet if trouble developed, George shoots Lennie to save him from a mob bent on lynching. Even the man who has achieved a certain amount of control over his instincts and his fellow man and who has shaped a dream—like George—is helpless in the hands of an indifferent and imperfect nature. In the terms that Warwick Wadlington suggests in "Pathos and Dreiser," we would have to argue that both *In Dubious Battle* and *Of Mice and Men*—like most of the stories in *The Long Valley*—are "pathetic" rather than "tragic." "In tragedy," Wadlington contends, "our attention is focused upon a man who suffers disjunction within himself; in pathos, more upon a man who suffers disjunction with his world." The fates of Pepé and Doc Burton and George and Lennie are forced upon them by a "world they never made." Only Danny in *Tortilla Flat* suffers internal disjunction.

Of Mice and Men, however, is Steinbeck's last work to end on such a note of hopeless resignation. With *The Grapes of Wrath,* his work undergoes a change. I suspect that this novel was originally to be as darkly pessimistic as its immediate predecessors. Steinbeck wrote his publishers that the first version (called "L'Affaire Lettuceberg") was "full of tricks to make people ridiculous." He refused even to let the publishers see the manuscript and instead exhausted himself by completely rewriting the work. By September, 1938, he was able to report that the new title would be *The Grapes of Wrath.* In *John Steinbeck,* I trace the way in which this novel portrays "the education of the heart" by showing the Joad family developing from a proud, irresponsible "fambly," "like a bunch of cows, when the lobos are ranging" into members of one vast human family that, in Preacher Casy's words, shares "one big soul ever'body's a part of."

The key to Steinbeck's changed attitude is an editorial in chapter 14:

> This you may say of man—when theories change and crash, when schools, philosophies, when narrow dark alleys of thought, national, religious, economic, grow and disintegrate, man reaches, stumbles forward, painfully, mistakenly sometimes. Having stepped forward, he may slip back, but only half a step, never the full step back. . . . And this you can know—fear the time when Manself will not suffer and die for a concept, for this one quality is the foundation of Manself, and this one quality is man, distinctive in the universe.

This credo is to underlie Steinbeck's fiction for the rest of his life and finds its final embodiment in these words from his Nobel Prize acceptance speech, "I hold that a writer who does not passionately believe in the perfectibility of man has no dedication nor any membership in literature."

The writer of *In Dubious Battle* and *Of Mice and Men* gave no evidence of believing in the perfectibility of man; such a concept is totally irreconcilable with the naturalistic theory that characters are "conditioned and controlled by environment, heredity, instinct or chance." When Steinbeck speaks of man as "distinctive in the universe," he is no longer talking about Stephen Crane's "blistered and sweating animals." *The Grapes of Wrath* is not a "naturalistic" novel; in Tom's final explanation to Ma that maybe it doesn't matter whether she knows where he is or not, because "If Casy knowed," "I'll be all aroun' in the dark," it becomes much more nearly supernaturalitic.

Steinbeck never again abandoned the position that he embraced in rewriting *The Grapes of Wrath*. Generally his post-World-War-II novels lack the vividness and immediacy of his earlier writings. This is not the place to explore his reputed "decline," because the novels following *The Grapes of Wrath* are in no sense "naturalistic," although it might be appropriate to suggest that his principal problem seems to have been to find stories that effectively dramatize affirmations. As I have commented in *American Winners of the Nobel Prize in Literature,*

> if the writer-critic is to make a valid and useful criticism of society, he must create characters who are not individuals in quest of unique identities, but allegorical representatives of mankind as a whole. He must create a convincingly specific

situation that mirrors a recognizably general one. . . . Steinbeck
has had quite uneven success in achieving this difficult fusion.

To show how far Steinbeck moved from the "naturalistic" conception
of character, I conclude with a pivotal passage from *East of Eden* (1952), in
which a character reports on the meaning of the Hebrew word "timshel"
that has been discussed at length in the novel and that Steinbeck carved
into the lid of the box in which he kept the manuscript. Following a report
from some elderly Chinese savants, Lee, a Chinese houseman, sums the
matter up:

> "The American Standard [Bible] translation *orders* men to
> triumph over sin, and you can call sin ignorance. The King
> James translation gives a promise in 'Thou shalt,' meaning that
> men will surely triumph over sin. But the Hebrew word, the
> word *timshel*—'Thou mayest'—that gives a choice. It might be
> the most important word in the world. That says the way is
> open. That throws it right back on a man. For if 'Thou
> mayest'—it is also true that 'Thou mayest not.' "

Stagey as this outburst sounds, it would be hard to construct a
statement that would more clearly contrast the deterministic and anti-
deterministic, the naturalistic and anti-naturalistic positions. Whatever one
may think of Steinbeck's post-World-War-II novels, they are definitely not
naturalistic, as his work of the 1930s had been. A concept, however, of the
naturalistic novel's focusing upon characters controlled by outside forces
instead of controlling them provides a clearly defined basis for distinguishing three markedly different periods in the career of one of the United
States's Nobel Prize winners in literature.

Obviously there was some correlation between the shifts in Steinbeck's views and events transpiring in the world around him. His works
were cynical dramas of consciousness before the stock market crash of
1929 precipitated the Depression. He produced his naturalistic works
during the 1930s, but he was shaken out of the pessimistic viewpoint
undergirding them in 1938 as the world moved toward war. Apparently
from his observations during and after World War II, he reached the
conclusion that man must take responsibility for his actions and that man is
capable—however reluctantly—of accepting this responsibility.

ARTHUR F. KINNEY

Tortilla Flat *Re-Visited*

*"Where is Arthur Morales?" Danny asked, turning his palms
up and thrusting his arms forward. "Dead in France," he
answered himself, turning the palms down and dropping
his arms in despair. "Dead for his country. Dead in a foreign
land."*

—Tortilla Flat

What is most troublesome about *Tortilla Flat* is the tone, "its grave and
playful cadences" as Joseph Warren Beach has it. We cannot divorce
undistanced sentiment from detached burlesque. Realism and fantasy
intertwine. The perspective shifts and blurs even in the preface where
Steinbeck addresses us directly.

> This is the story of Danny and of Danny's friends and of
> Danny's house. It is a story of how these three became one
> thing, so that in Tortilla Flat if you speak of Danny's house you
> do not mean a structure of wood flaked with old whitewash,
> overgrown with an ancient untrimmed rose of Castile. No,
> when you speak of Danny's house you are understood to mean
> a unit of which the parts are men, from which came sweetness
> and joy, philanthropy and, in the end, a mystic sorrow.

From a real place, a shanty sociologically accurate, the perspective glides
almost imperceptibly into exaggerated storytelling, inviting us to formulate
a legend centered in "mystic sorrow," yet the whole tale, Steinbeck contin-

From *Steinbeck and the Arthurian Theme*, edited by Tetsumaro Hayashi. Steinbeck
Monograph Series no. 5, 1975. © 1975 by Tetsumaro Hayashi. The John Steinbeck Society of America, 1975.

ues, is true and his facts will so ground the story of Danny that his "history" will "now and ever . . . keep the sneers from the lips of sour scholars." Thus we are carried from realism through fantasy to admitting a parody of both.

Our difficulties are only compounded as we read on. We are continually frustrated by wide and erratic shifts from the meanness and poverty of the *paisanos* to the exaggerated claims Steinbeck insists on or implies for them; inconsistencies are in the very fabric of each episode. The novel opens with Danny's return to Monterey from Army service, his inheritance of two houses, and his flight from this responsibility. He gets drunk but he does not resist arrest, nor does he pillory the justice of the peace who sentences him or the police who charge him because "He had a vast respect for the law." Yet this model citizen escapes from jail at the first opportunity, "determined to hide all day to escape pursuit," and at night this model citizen steals "two slices of ham, four eggs, a lamb chop, and a fly swatter," cheating a benefactor who has momentarily left to fetch him a handout of bread. Irresolution rests too where we seem to hear Steinbeck clearly as artist: the man he names Pilon—"something thrown in when a trade is conducted," an accessory—emerges as the central actor, both chief rationalizer, as when he suggests that Danny rent one house to pay for another, and chief mystic, as in his apostrophe to the heavens. It is Pilon we come to believe in locating the attractiveness and the limitations of the paisanos, for it is he who thinks and reveals most as Steinbeck's commentator, yet it is also Pilon who steals Mrs. Morales's chickens as if he were hunting down dangerous game and kills the bird in an act of pretended euthanasia. Handy dandy, who is the victim and who is the thief? When—and what—are we to believe? Is this novel about self-rationalizing, self-deluded confidence men only itself the best con job of them all, with us its ultimate targets?

If this were true, we could dismiss Steinbeck's novel as a rather splendid joke, an exercise in folk comedy or, at worst, in romantic nostalgia for a more simplified if remote existence. Yet this is precisely what we are unable to do. The disturbing and haunting qualities of *Tortilla Flat*— what leads Maxwell Geismar to see only a "perplexing *appearance* of serenity"—derives from matters grave enough that the most serious among us is invited to evasion. For in the story Steinbeck himself tells us, it is not freedom, property, nor responsibility which destroys Danny and his circle— that is *their* communal illusion, *their* stay against mortality as we shall see shortly—but the persistent fear of a man's vulnerability. What forces Danny to his harrowing final self-confrontation are two incidents of hu-

youth and beauty and the corporal's baby who shrivels and dies before his eyes, and ours too, as the corporal spins out his own romantic fantasy of suicidal self-delusion. It is revealing that, as Peter Lisca long ago told us, these are the two factual incidents around which *Tortilla Flat* was conceived. The self-consciousness Steinbeck betrays of his own fictionalizing, this discomforting medley of tones, intimates what remains unspoken at the end: that the legend, the sentiment, and the burlesque are all present to conceal the ultimate terror of death which always lurks at the edge of the narrative.

Such nervous laughter was not uncommon among Steinbeck's own colleagues; we see it in Don Marquis and Ring Lardner, for example. But it is most instructive in understanding the Steinbeckian perspective to see its affinity to the work of Malory where Steinbeck repeatedly refers us. For as with Malory, so with Steinbeck: the outer form of Danny's band, his *comitatus,* like its inner spirit of shared rationalizations and self-deceptions, is a form of group survival. The ritual, however parodied, nevertheless maintains a strength of resistance against a commercialized society which the paisanos see as powerful and predatory, a society which robs them of the liberty and self-indulgence which constitutes their only recognizable form of selfhood yet paradoxically encourages their essential dependence on each other. It is just such a counter-society, a *counter-culture,* that the *Morte d'Arthur* celebrates, for Arthur's Round Table is, beneath the glitter of tournaments and the romance of chivalry, a structure which contains, directs, and so sustains forces that guarantee its own preservation against the semi-mythical sinister forces. "Malory is careful," [Eugène] Vinaver reminds us, to show us Arthur "not as a mere abstract centre of the fellowship of the Round Table, but as a political and military leader, conscious of his responsibility for the welfare and the prestige of his kingdom." To sense how power alone inspires and insures Arthur's rule, we have only to recall Layamon's account of how the Table Round began amidst the slaughter of anarchic rebels from Britain, Scotland, and Ireland, and Iceland, and Arthur's threats of vengeance through execution or maiming; and how it ended, according to Geoffrey of Monmouth, writing still earlier, in the "defence of a narrow place against insurmountable odds." That Malory overlaid the savagery of tribal warfare with a veneer of French courtly romance in the *Morte* only shows the persistent pressures of his own eschatological vision. For the unresolved perspective that so bothers us in Steinbeck was already present in Malory. "Through much of it," E. K. Chambers says of the *Morte d'Arthur* sadly, "we walk perplexedly."

II

"Fact and fiction, romantic impossibility and historical likelihood, are intertwined at many stages of Arthurian story," John Lawlor writes. Malory, too, marries the comfortable fabulous with the grievous actual. In his astonishing adeptness at synthesizing the chronicle histories of Arthur and his battles, the amorous adventures of Lancelot, and the mystical aspirations of Percival and Galahad and Bors and the search for the Grail which he got from sources as discordant as Geoffrey of Monmouth, Layamon, Wace, the Vulgate Cycle, and Chrétien, there is in Malory a symphony of tones both wide-ranging and restless.

In Geoffrey of Monmouth Malory found a description of the Island of Apples,

> which men call the Fortunate Isle, . . . so named became it produces all things without toil. The fields there have no need of farmers to plough them, and Nature alone provides the tilling. Grain and grapes are produced without tending, and apple-trees grow in the woods from the close-clipped grass.
>
> (*Life of Merlin*)

Here in a land reminiscent of the Tortilla Flat section of Monterey, Geoffrey has the wounded Arthur transported after the battle of Camlan. It is a land hugely at odds with England, as Tortilla Flat is at odds with the city below it, and disjunctive too with the sense of doom (Saxon *faege*, Middle English *feye*, Scots *fey*) that saturates the story of Arthur in two other of Malory's sources, in Layamon and Wace. In subsequent accounts of Arthur the primitive savagery of the Round Table is openly declared. Layamon's Arthur threatens to burn Guenevere as his Gawain proposes that she be torn to pieces by horses (there is "a Nazi streak of ruthlessness and cruelty in Layamon," [Roger Sherman] Loomis tells us with almost admirable reticence [in *The Development of Arthurian Romance*]); in the Vulgate Cycle, chivalric tournaments continually erupt into bitter battles and sieges. Malory developed a number of responses to such cruelty. In the mysterious Grail which floats through the great hall of the Fisher King in the Vulgate Cycle (as well as in the mysterious chalice which keeps refilling itself like a horn of plenty with foodstuffs, perhaps a distant source for the Pirate's daily round of miraculous handouts in preparation for his own approaching vision of Saint Francisco) we find a faltering attempt to overcome through magic and mystery the pervasive sense of fate which outweighs the forces of the Table Round's best dreams.

More disparate and less easily accounted for is Chrétien's response to the unspeakable brutality in Layamon and Wace. Chrétien burlesques Lancelot. Here the knight is carried to extreme frenzy and to extreme humiliation: he almost swoons over a comb he finds beside a spring which contains strands of the Queen's hair, and he presses the hairs to his eyes, mouth, and forehead a hundred thousand times before depositing them under his shirt next to his heart. At another point he so loses himself in thinking of his lady that a knight challenges him three times and unhorses him into a ford before he comes to his senses. Later on, hearing a false rumor of Guenevere's death, he attempts to hang himself unsuccessfully. While admittedly many medieval readers "took these aberrancies rather solemnly," Loomis comments, "Chrétien was far too sane. His Lancelot is a caricature, a Don Quixote," and potential ancestor of Pilon, the Pirate, and (most notably) Big Joe Portagee.

In examining Malory we witness not only the different tones we see so peculiarly elided in *Tortilla Flat,* but we find Malory's means of synthesis illuminating. His fundamental unity is of the broadest sort: in an imposed atmosphere jointly romantic and moralizing; in the celebration of the past through unremitting and untarnished praise of the ideals of knighthood; in a focus on a half-dozen characters who develop biographically from the idealism of youth to the jaded disillusionment of old age. Thus the rise, flowering, and fall of the Round Table serves Malory as an overarching metaphor for the biographies of men, of dreams, and of society generally. The apparently discrete episodes, the occasional interruption of time for what R. H. Wilson calls "looping back" or what R. M. Lumiansky has termed "retrospective narrative" in order to give the early accounts of Percival and Galahad (much as Steinbeck impedes the flow of his narrative with the inserted story of the corporal or the old suitor who hanged himself and the early accounts of Jesus Maria, Big Joe, and Danny), build through accretion to a heightened sense of the awful loss of a past time which is the chief burden of the present. The literary strategies which Malory derives from others or creates himself to preserve nostalgia keep countering an irrevocable despair. Even the panels of knightly adventures meant to reify and so reassert the good times of happier past are defeated at every turn by concordant omens and forecasts of unavoidable doom. Romance finally surrenders to this didacticism of fate.

"Like the Bible," Loomis reminds us, "the *Book of King Arthur and His Noble Knights* is an assemblage of materials from different peoples and epochs, and looks at life from shifting points of view. There is a fascination in watching the kaleidoscopic changes in colour and dominant pattern as one passes from tale to tale." Yet these too seem self-conscious on Malory's part, seem openly aware that fiction has become not merely an agent for recalling the past but a defense, itself the only means of establishing, however tentatively, a past that can no longer plead authentic belief and testimonial. For example, Malory draws on the Vulgate Cycle for his most daring act of synthesis, the begetting of Galahad by Lancelot on the daughter of the Grail King by which, as Jean Frappier first observed, "the mystic part of the cycle is indissolubly linked to the profane." Here and elsewhere in an intensification of the mysterious Malory reaches out in a last effort to rescue his ideals from the fiction that threatens to make them coterminous with itself.

The reason for Malory's uneasiness is plain enough: the story he must tell (but keeps putting off) is not that of the Golden Age of English history as he hollowly proclaims but, as D. S. Brewer remarks, "how it came to its tragic end." The tension in Malory, imprisoned as he read and wrote, is that in spite of his most superhuman efforts to bring courage, trust, and heroism to the middle of his tale, he could not prevent its tragic conclusion. The omens of fate could at any moment defeat the idealism of his heroes and the fondest wishes of his own most considered fiction. We have "entered a region," as C. S. Lewis remarks of Malory, "where even what is best and greatest by the common standards of the world 'falls into abatement and low price' "; the battle for Malory (as for Steinbeck) was lost before it really began. It is the downward movement of Fortune's wheel which alone gains momentum throughout the last three books of Malory; it is the adversity of unavoidable defeat which proves strongest. Just as Steinbeck's restlessness stems from the terror of death, Malory's grows out of the terror he intimates but can never pronounce. Behind even the grandest of adventures in Malory lurks the spectre of futility.

III

There is no necessity to trace exact correspondences for Steinbeck's characters and episodes in Malory nor even to determine the degree of influence; what the affinity alerts us to is a sharper appreciation for Steinbeck's discordances. They stem from whatever he—and through him the paisanos—are, openly or not, finally unwilling to face. With the paisanos it is their own selfishness and savagery that lie concealed during their moments of self-control. Their fear of treachery or even of self-betrayal explodes in their extreme punishment of Big Joe, action altogether out of proportion to his crime.

Danny leaned down, took him by the shoulder, and rolled him over on his face. Then the friends went over his back with the same deadly precision. The cries grew weaker, but the work only stopped when Big Joe was beaten into unconsciousness. Then Pilon tore off the blue shirt and exposed the pulpy raw back. With the can-opener he cross-hatched the skin so deftly that a little blood ran from each line. Pablo brought the salt to him and helped him to rub it in all over the torn back. At last Danny threw a blanket over the unconscious man.

The gratuitousness of Pilon and Pablo is what shocks us most, what shows their own temptation and inner self-hatred as they see it mirrored in Big Joe's theft. But it is not unprepared for. We have witnessed the hard fights of the paisanos; we have even heard how Cornelia Ruiz cut up a persistent suitor. Caught or threatened, the paisanos can become animalistic: greedy, lusting, vengeful; and their game of brotherhood repeatedly stands displayed as the fiction it is.

The comitatus is their chief ritual, but there are others: the sharing of grappa, the privacy of sexual affairs, the pretense to morality and guilt (as in burning down Danny's house). Their counter-culture is reinforced through their joint attack on the capitalistic society which surrounds them and which, in its advocacy of property and its insistence on unalterable responsibility, challenges them with its own enduring vitality. But what the Christian communism of the paisanos masks is their own capitalistic proclivity. It is not true, finally, that the paisanos combat capitalism or absorb its ways unknowingly; what we come to learn is that they actively embrace it. The satire on greed for treasure which is the focus of the St. Andrew's Eve ritual and the motivating force for Pilon and Big Joe is only the most obvious satiric instance of this; we misunderstand the paisanos seriously if we forget that it is acquisition of a vacuum cleaner that wins Teresa Ramirez for Danny and earns her social status among other paisanos—and which Danny *also* admires as he purchases it; it is the gift of wine (not love or companionship) that Pilon and Pablo use to buy Danny's friendship (as it was his house that attracted them to him in the first place); and it is a brassiere that Big Joe plans to use in bribing Arabella Gross and that Pilon appropriates to bribe Danny. Bribery and extortion characterize the paisanos' relationship with Torelli and with his wife Butter Duck. It is what he owned that distinguished Danny's grandfather, the old *viejo,* that awakened Mrs. Morales's interest in Danny, and (as Steinbeck himself comments) creates Danny's comitatus, his very selfhood: synonymously, *Tortilla*

Flat does remain, as it begins, "the story of Danny and of Danny's friends and of Danny's house." The constant talk of Danny's house and the constant devaluation of it only reveals how important the residence is to the paisanos who live there. And it is monetary gain (and surely not the sport of locating it or spending it on wine alone) that first calls the paisanos' attention to the Pirate.

But the Pirate comes to represent a danger of the capitalism against which the paisanos do protest too much. He is a hoarder; his little mound of hidden money is only the obvious analogue for Danny's second house and for the bottles and foodstuffs which the paisanos habitually hide in their pockets and coats, hide *from one another*. Their claim to pride is their claim to possessing something someone else wants; their chief despair is the frustration of not getting what someone else has. Capitalists at heart, they shun the Monterey fishermen who are chronic victims of capitalistic frustration throughout the novel—"Those lonely fishermen who believe that the fish bite at high tide left their rocks, and their places were taken by others who were convinced that the fish bite at low tide"—yet the resilient desire of these fishermen only circumscribes an aching but unspoken desire of the paisanos to be well supplied with the good things of life. Their fear of losing what little they own haunts them and explains why they fear Big Joe as a kind of nemesis whose presence awakens in them their own sense of greedy possessiveness. It is in these terms that the suicidal father and the corporal's dying son test them, for both also indicate the drive to ownership, the old man Ravanno wanting to own Tonia, the sister of his son's wife, the baby the victim of his father's concern with wealth and status rather than his child's health. Capitalism is thus paradoxical in *Tortilla Flat* as the paisanos come dimly to sense and Danny openly to acknowledge: while ownership provides self-realization and the respect from others, it also betokens its own finite existence—and hence in miniature emblemizes the finitude, the mortality, of man himself.

It is against this shadowy awareness of disaster and self-betrayal (the paisanos' values leading to a larger scene of suicide) that Danny and his friends compound their humor and nostalgia, their rituals and their undefined mysticism; and it is this that makes the Pirate (with his visions) so precious to them just as it makes Big Joe so momentous a threat. It is in such defenses that they can muster, too, that Steinbeck displays his own immense gift at folk humor—for we can never forget that *Tortilla Flat* is, in many ways, a very funny book. There are the broad farces—Teresa's pride in a vacuum cleaner which impresses a neighborhood without electricity; the theft of Big Joe's pants and their return; the furious hunt after a geodetic survey marker—and there are also the gentler parodies: the vision of St. Francis expended on the Pirate's dogs; the oversupplying of food to Teresina ("Mrs. Cortez") and her eight children. The festive imagination of the paisanos in story-telling, the zest of their scavenging, even the vitality of their mystical explanations of St. Andrew's Eve and of the cause of the fire that destroys Danny's first house are themselves so wonderful, so entertaining, so diverting, that we too forget momentarily that they keep us from the main business of life as they protect the paisanos from the main threat to theirs.

It is all a very funny mirage, and we should not be surprised that everyone knows it. Mrs. Morales has no interest in Danny once he loses one of his houses; even Sweets grows disinterested once she loses her vacuum cleaner (as the other paisanos anticipate). Yet these moments of dismay are slight indications of the pervasive view that life itself is a falling off, a progressive loss which in their more confessional moments these paisanos come to admit. When Pilon and Pablo first retire to their house in triumph, having their own shelter together at last, their second bottle of wine reveals this to them.

> They moved on to the next graduation, and Pilon remembered how happy he had been when he was a little boy. "No care then, Pablo. I knew not sin. I was very happy."
> "We have never been happy since," Pablo agreed sadly.

When we encounter this scene, at the quiet closing of chapter 3, we find its disharmony unsettling but chalk it up to drunken sentimentality, another exaggeration of inebriated nostalgia. But it persists, as counterstatement that will not go away. We meet with it again in chapter 8 after the joke with the geodetic survey marker; again through drink Pilon's summary observation jolts us in its repetitive aptness: " 'How we build,' Pilon cried. 'How our dreams lead us.' " We are therefore, quietly yet securely, prepared for the entrance of the corporal at the hands of the charitable but inept Jesus Maria Corcoran, and the slow painful death of the corporal's baby and prepared, through that, to the larger significance of the death-in-life of the Ravanno family. We learn of this as Pilon's morbid awareness—not unlike the sense of *ubi sunt* that filters everywhere through Malory—passes from Pilon to Jesus Maria himself.

> "Well," said Jesus Maria, "I will tell you that story, and you will see if you can laugh. When I was a little boy, I played games with Petey Ravanno. A good quick little boy, that Petey,

but always in trouble. He had two brothers and four sisters, and there was his father, Old Pete. All that family is gone now. One brother is in San Quentin, the other was killed by a Japanese gardener for stealing a wagonload of watermelons. And the girls, well, you know how girls are; they went away. Susy is in Old Jenny's house in Salinas right now."

Yes, we like the paisanos know—have known all along—how girls are, but this reference has taken a somber turn. Even the interlude of Petey's staged suicide to win Gracie Montez (for we also know how boys are) ends in the sobering, because irredeemable, suicide of Old Petey his father. The horror is further underlined for us because unlike Jesus Maria but like Pilon we see its bitter analogies to the incident recounted in chapter 7.

Pilon began it. "I had an uncle, a regular miser, and he hid his gold in the woods. And one time he went to look at it, and it was gone. Someone had found it and stolen it. He was an old man, then, and all his money was gone, and he hanged himself."

The equation of money and life foreshadows the incidents of the corporal's baby, of Old Petey, and finally of Danny himself.

In *Tortilla Flat* Danny first links the unspoken capitalism of the paisanos with their silent fears of the uncontrollable, who sees his clinging to a house (or a vacuum cleaner) as deliberately self-delusive. "Danny began to feel the beating of time." His break with his friends and his house is thus his own wild attempt to find a freer, truer existence; his return a submission to failure, his confessional self-condemnation. He openly admits this in the recklessness that leads to his death; Steinbeck acknowledges it in the unconquerable sorrow at his funeral (itself a military parody of the sociological parody with which Steinbeck opens chapter 17); the paisanos recognize it, too, forced to view the funeral from across the street without appropriate clothes that, like their dreams, parody the capitalism they cherish from afar; later, they burn Danny's remaining house, sole remaining foundation for their materialistic and brotherly band, in an unspoken pact of joint suicide. The general despair in the concluding moments of *Tortilla Flat* is neither disjunctive in tone nor unpredictable in structure; and it results not from the death of Danny (whom the paisanos had not missed when he was away in the Army) nor by the restraints of civilization (which they imitated rather than avoided), but by their honest self-measurement of their inadequacies before the forces of life itself. Maxwell Geismar sensed that too some years back, though not in *Tortilla*

Flat; "Steinbeck . . . identifies himself," Geismar tells us of Steinbeck's later work, "not merely with the pleasures of the dispossessed . . . but with their needs." The grave matter beneath the high good spirits of the paisanos is their hesitation before the fears of total self-revelation and of mortality we all share—and that Steinbeck shares, too, with Malory.

IV

The frequent charge of softness in the Steinbeck of *Tortilla Flat,* the complaint that "his reliance on rhapsody rather than reflection" betrays an unacceptable superficiality, shows a failure of nerve before the paisanos, for they manage their meager existence by fashioning a finer life from the imagination. Their devotion to fable as a means of making do is the source of our joy in them as, centuries earlier in our culture, the English and French took their joy in Arthur. About this Malory is as clear as Steinbeck. "Wyte you well," Malory's Arthur announces,

> my harte was never so hevy as hit ys now. And much more I am soryar for my good knyghtes losse than for the losse of my fayre quene; for quenys I myght have inow, but such felyship of good knyghtes shall never be togydirs in no company.

The means by which we achieve the good life in our fantasies are inter-changeable counters; but we shall risk everything before the loss of the final resource of such necessary dreaming. Clearly this is why Malory mustered all his own strength while in prison to recharge the formal and futile tournaments of his sources with a new life and power and why he assigned his own private sustenance to a way of life the fourteenth century had already underscored as essentially futile. The civil war which under-mines Arthur's Round Table is not only the inner decay of an extenuated and so decadent society but the decay of the soul of man—and against this Malory shores up all the romance his "Fressh bookes" can summon to him. The ineluctable Fates, the retributive sense of justice, the need to punish the stubborn and selfish knights of the Table Round (including Arthur) for their pride and circumscribed courage are all openly admitted by Malory while the possibility of Arthur's resurrection still holds out a compensatory hope, a renewed resource for faith in man and in his unreal-ized greatness. In the end, in Malory's incompleteness, "we are left with a kingdom and the values it epitomized breached from within," (Lawlor) but we are not rendered altogether helpless. In the strange medieval confusion of *fabula* and *historia*—something Cicero, who defined the terms, could

never have accomplished, nor any of the Greek and Roman historians
before or after—Malory admits to man's mortality even as he admits the
possibility of *im*mortality. As if in deliberate parallel,

> "Where is Arthur Morales?" Danny asked, turning his palms
> up and thrusting his arms forward. "Dead in France," he
> answered himself, turning the palms down and dropping his
> arms in despair. "Dead for his country. Dead in a foreign land.
> Strangers walk near his grave and they do not know Arthur
> Morales lies there." He raised his hands palms upward again.
> "Where is Pablo, that good man?"

At its most literal application, Arthur Morales's death frees his widow for
Danny; but *Tortilla Flat* will take us beyond that restricted moment. It
takes us even here, with Danny, past Arthur's death to Pablo's living; and
this adumbrates the moment when we must move past Danny's death to
Pablo's destruction of the house that was their life together—to the living
Pablo, also suicidal yet also, in the final pages, not certainly dead. In
Steinbeck Arthur Morales and Danny do not *surely* die, just as in Malory
King Arthur—we have the daring right to hope—still lives in Avalon.
Logically, this denies all the honest confrontation with mortality and all
the forthright sorrow that precedes Arthur's departure and Danny's funeral; but in both books, which with equal honesty confront the necessity
of fiction, this hope held out for the resurrection of an Arthur or a Danny
is the only adequate conclusion to the compensating countertheme. For
both achievements are signalled by their open marriage of *historia* and
fabula.

    In getting at this true illogicality in Malory, Larry D. Benson recalls
Richard Hurd in the eighteenth century on Spenser's *Faerie Queene*:
"Judge the Fairy Queen by the classic models, and you are shocked by its
disorder; consider it with an eye to its Gothic originals and you find it
regular." By analogy, judge *Tortilla Flat* by *Main Street* or *Martin Eden*
and we will be bewildered and irritated by its apparent sentimentality and
burlesque and disturbed by its inconsistent attitudes and discordant tones;
judge it by Malory's *Morte d'Arthur* and we shall be saddened by its world
of imagination lost forever and its awareness of human greed, savagery,
and mortality. Judge it, finally, by its admission of our need for sentimentality and our sometimes desperate uses of burlesque—by its courting of a
necessary fiction—and we will not only find it meaningful: we shall also
find the ideational and artistic progenitor of *The Grapes of Wrath*.

MARILYN L. MITCHELL

Steinbeck's Strong Women: Feminine Identity in the Short Stories

Most writers of the first half of this century concentrated on character-izations of men and the problems and motivations of men. Perhaps that is because most writers of anything other than romantic novels or popular magazine stories were men. Two notable exceptions to the pattern were John Steinbeck and D. H. Lawrence, who tried to release woman from the pasteboard, shadowy role she generally assumed in fiction. Today, Law-rence's portraits of aggressive and often neurotic women have come under attack by certain feminist critics, while Steinbeck's contributions to Ameri-can literature in any sense are ignored or dismissed. Mention of Steinbeck recalls only *The Grapes of Wrath,* a powerful social work but not his best literary achievement, nor the one in which he demonstrated greatest sensi-tivity to female characters. True, Ma Joad and Rosasharn are unforgetta-ble women, but both clearly fall into the "earth-mother" category which is a stereotype, however flattering. Rather than in this novel or his others from the thirties, it is in his short stories that Steinbeck's understanding of his craft and of women is to be found.

Two of John Steinbeck's more intricate and memorable stories in *The Long Valley* are "The Chrysanthemums" and "The White Quail." Both examine the psychology and sexuality of strong women who must some-how express themselves meaningfully within the narrow possibilities open to women in a man's world. In each case the woman chooses a traditional feminine activity, gardening, as a creative outlet, yet the dedication with

From *Southwest Review* 61, no. 3 (Summer 1976). © 1976 by Marilyn L. Mitchell.

which each undertakes her project is of the sort traditionally considered masculine. It is the conflict between society's view of what constitutes masculinity and its view of what constitutes femininity as well as the conflict between the women and men depicted which carries the action and determines the development of character. In addition, Steinbeck reveals fundamental differences between the way women see themselves and the way they are viewed by men. For example, both husbands relate primarily to the physical attributes of their wives, making only meager attempts to comprehend their personalities. Consequently, a gulf of misunderstanding exists between the marriage partners which creates verbal as well as sexual blocks to communication. In each marriage at least one of the spouses is aware of some degree of sexual frustration, although dissatisfaction is never overtly articulated. Furthermore, the propensity of the men to see their wives as dependent inferiors, while the women perceive themselves as being equal if not superior partners, creates a strain within the marriage which is partially responsible for the isolation of each of the characters.

Both Elisa Allen of "The Chrysanthemums" and Mary Teller in "The White Quail" display a strength of will usually identified with the male but which, in these cases, the husbands are not shown to have. Steinbeck's women, with their rather bisexual identities, naturally recall certain female characters created by D. H. Lawrence, notably Gudrun Brangwen in *Women in Love* and March in "The Fox." Critics Richard F. Peterson [in *Steinbeck's Literary Dimension,* edited by Tetsumaro Hayashi] and Peter Lisca [in *The Wide World of John Steinbeck*] have also noted the similarity between Steinbeck and Lawrence in the "psychological portraits of frustrated females," (Lisca) but decline to draw parallels between specific characters. They imply, however, that such frustration is due to an incapacity for sexual response on the part of the women.

Elisa Allen demonstrates a very earthy sensuality in "The Chrysanthemums," though not in the presence of her husband, indicating that their failure as a couple may be as much his fault as hers. Mary Teller, on the other hand, is frigid, yet she responds orgasmically to the sight of the white quail: "A shiver of pleasure, a bursting of pleasure swelled in Mary's breast. She held her breath. . . . A powerful ecstasy quivered in her body." But Mary's response is really triggered by the experience of seeing herself in another form and is therefore autoerotic:

> "Why," Mary cried to herself, "She's like me! . . . She's like
> the essence of me, an essence boiled down to utter purity. She

must be the queen of the quail. She makes every lovely thing that ever happened to me one thing. . . . This is the me that was everything beautiful. This is the center of me, my heart."

Mary has a physical dimension, but she does not respond to that which is foreign to her, i.e., the male, her husband, who in turn tolerates her coldness, assuming that good women are naturally a bit repelled by sex. He understood that "there were things Mary didn't like to talk about. The lock on her bedroom door was an answer to a question, a clean, quick, decisive answer." Because he cannot force his will on her—she had married him for that reason—his frustration in the marriage will remain unvoiced, to be given expression only symbolically in his deliberate murder of her surrogate self, the white quail.

"The White Quail" is as fabulous and ethereal in dialogue and setting as "The Chrysanthemums" is naturalistic. Furthermore, Steinbeck has created in Elisa Allen a warm, three-dimensional character with whom the reader can identify, just as he has made Mary Teller a virtual caricature of the selfish, castrating female who inspires animosity. The only obvious connection one woman has with the other is the superficial but significant detail that Mary and Elisa are childless women who have transferred maternal impulses to a garden. In addition, however, both women are trapped between society's definition of the masculine and the feminine and are struggling against the limitations of the feminine. That struggle is more apparent in the life of Elisa Allen than in that of Mary Teller, who is more physically fragile. Yet Mary is one of the most ruthless and egotistical of all Steinbeck's characters, although outwardly she conforms to the stereotype of feminine weakness. Her mythic depiction in a story that is practically a fable in modern dress leads one to conclude that Steinbeck is using her to refute outmoded conceptions of what a woman should be. Mary is not Steinbeck's model of the wife; she is merely Elisa's opposite who serves to show the real human beauty beneath Elisa's rough and somewhat masculine exterior.

Steinbeck introduces the reader to the narrow world of Mary Teller's garden through a dormer window composed of leaded, diamond-shaped panes. The convex curvature of the window and the fragmentation of its space indicate that the vision of the person within, Mary Teller, is distorted. Having been thoroughly acquainted with the landscaping and contents of the garden, we are finally, in the third paragraph, introduced to Mary, "Mrs. Harry E. Teller, that is." In the last paragraph of part 1, Steinbeck again uses Mary's name, followed by her husband's, to show that it is her vision which controls the story. For five years she had looked for the man who would construct the garden she had so meticulously planned. "When she met Harry Teller, the garden seemed to like him." Personification of the garden reveals that to Mary it is a "child" whose "step-father" she must carefully select with only a secondary interest in the man's desirability as a husband.

Harry, of course, has no understanding of Mary's personality or motivations, nor does he believe any is necessary. Just as she is attracted to him for his passivity and his income, so he is attracted to her for her apparent delicacy and beauty: "You're so pretty. You make me kind of—hungry." Her attractiveness will also make her an asset to his business: "He was proud of her when people came to dinner. She was so pretty, so cool and perfect." And since he does not expect a pretty girl to have any dimension but the physical, the firm determination with which she engineers the garden's construction comes as a surprise to him: "Who could tell that such a pretty girl could have so much efficiency." His misconception of women is largely responsible for Mary's success in completely dominating him, for she skillfully cloaks her aggressive manipulations in feminine frailty.

For her part, Mary is dedicated to the impossible task of creating something perfect, a beautiful reflection of herself which will remain forever unchanged. As the workmen finish landscaping, she says to her husband: "We won't ever change it, will we, Harry? If a bush dies, we'll put another one just like it in the same place. . . . If anything should be changed it would be like part of me being torn out." But neither the garden nor Mary's life can be completely perfect, because there are always dangers in the world waiting to destroy the beautiful. The threat to the garden comes from the wild foliage of the hill which would destroy its order and serenity were it not for the sturdy but exotic line of fuchsias, "little symbolic trees," obviously representing Mary. The hill too is a symbol—a symbol for everything which is not Mary. It, like Harry, opposes the irrationality of feeling and happenstance to her unemotional rationality.

Ironically perhaps, Mary's love for the garden does not imply a love of nature, for she reacts violently against the natural biological order which would alter her arrangement. Harry is appointed killer of the pests that come in the night to attack her garden, but, though he does not see it, she is the one who most relishes the slaughter:

> Mary held the flashlight while Harry did the actual killing, crushing the slugs and snails into oozy, bubbling masses. He

knew it must be a disgusting business to her, but the light never wavered. "Brave girl," he thought. "She has a sturdiness in back of that fragile beauty." She made the hunts exciting too. "There's a big one, creeping and creeping," she would say. "He's after that big bloom. Kill him! Kill him quickly!" They came into the house after the hunts laughing happily.

Harry, however, declines to kill other animals for her sake. Although he meekly accepts her absolute refusal to let him own a dog which might "do things on the plants in her garden, or even dig in her flower beds," he will not set out poison for the cat which had crept from the hill into her garden and was threatening the birds. He argues that "animals suffer terribly when they get poison," and despite Mary's indifference to that argument, he insists that an air rifle will work as an effective deterrent once the cat has been stung by a pellet. Harry may realize subconsciously that the cat is symbolic of him just as the white quail is of Mary. It is evident that Mary, at least, sees the cat as a threat to her: "That white quail was *me*, the secret me that no one can ever get at, the me that's way inside. . . . Can't you see, dear? The cat was after me. It was going to kill me. That's why I want to poison it."

Throughout the story, Harry's threat as husband to Mary's perfection has been made obvious. She locks her bedroom door against his advances to prevent his getting at "the me that's way inside." Of course, the phrase also applies to her actual personality, which he is equally unable to penetrate. Mary does not like dirt, rust, disorder, and slimy things like the slugs, all of which she perceives as concomitants of the sex act. Since her range of emotional expression is circumscribed by the limitations of the self, Harry's person and that which emanates from him are beyond her appreciation. Harry is as much an outsider in her world as the animals and the hill. To her, sex is not a sharing of physical and emotional energy, but rather a price she must pay for the garden. Four times, in describing Mary's response to Harry's advances, Steinbeck writes that "she let him." The phrase is used three times describing their courtship, and only once following the wedding, after which the locked door is mentioned on two occasions. Furthermore, it is significant that "the lot was bought and the house was built, and they were married," in that order. Afterward, Harry is not invited into the garden except on those occasions when he is to protect it from harm. He may admire it but not enjoy it in the twilight hours which are "almost a sacred time" for her. "When Harry came home from the office, he stayed in the house and read his paper until she came in from the garden, star-eyed. It made her unhappy to be disturbed." How she in any way, in fact, functions as wife to Harry is unclear, because even their dinner is prepared by another person, a high-school girl.

Just as Mary, inside, perceives the garden through a distorted glass, so her perception of the home, and the marriage, is distorted when she is outside looking in. She sees the living room "like a picture, like the set of a play that was about to start," and having noticed Harry, in passing, reading the paper, she conjures a vision of herself sitting in the firelight's glow in quiet perfection:

> She could almost see herself sitting there. Her round arms and long fingers were resting on the chair. Her delicate, sensitive face was in profile, looking reflectively into the firelight. "What is she thinking about?" Mary whispered. "I wonder what's going on in her mind. Will she get up? No, she's just sitting there. The neck of that dress is too wide, see how it slips sideways over the shoulder. But that's rather pretty. It looks careless, but neat and pretty. Now—she's smiling. She must be thinking something nice."

Harry is but a financial necessity in Mary Teller's world. In begging him to poison the cat, which opposes her will, she is obliquely threatening him as well, and he responds to her challenge by deliberately, though surreptitiously, killing the white quail with which she so strongly identified. This act of destruction, F. W. Watt writes in his *Steinbeck* (1967), is the result of the "sexual and intellectual gulf between a husband and wife." Although Harry has temporarily forsaken his passive role for action, it is not a constructive one and will bring no resolution. His last words in the story are, "I'm lonely. . . . Oh, Lord, I'm so lonely." In a sense, he has become the white quail, a pitiful victim, while the garden, the cat, and Mary continue to survive.

In this story, as in "The Chrysanthemums," Steinbeck proposes no solutions for the psychological conflicts which plague human interactions. There will always be predators and victims in life which is comprised of mere plateaus of contentment between joy and despair. Although Mary Teller, at story's end, is ignorant of the death of the quail, her period of happiness is nonetheless predestined to dissolution as are all the works of man. She cannot prevent the physical deterioration of her body or of the garden; then what will become of her self-admiration and her husband's love?

Elisa Allen of "The Chrysanthemums," whom Joseph W. Beach calls "one of the most delicious characters ever transferred from life to the pages of a book," is a vastly more sympathetic figure than Harry Teller but more akin to him in her loneliness and frustration than to his wife, Mary. Still she, like Mary, "mothers" a garden, a chrysanthemum bed, and takes great pride in her ability to nurture life and beauty. She says of her flowers, as if they were children, that "it's the budding that takes the most time." A similarity of setting is also notable. Elisa's house and garden, though not as spatially restricted as Mary Teller's, are proscribed areas of beauty and security which she maintains against the wilderness, yet without losing an appreciation for the wild beauty beyond her yard. Physically as well as emotionally, however, Elisa and Mary are almost complete opposites. Steinbeck continually refers to Mary as "pretty," but he describes Elisa's face as "eager and mature and handsome," interesting masculine adjectives. Mordecai Marcus is correct in saying in "The Lost Dream of Sex and Childbirth in 'The Chrysanthemums,' " that Elisa's "pervasive combination of femininity and masculinity" is an element "central to the story."

Another contrast is that, while Mary Teller's selfish refusal to compromise her ambitions recalls Gudrun Brangwen of *Women in Love,* who eventually destroyed her lover Gerald Crich, Elisa Allen's strength coupled with her vulnerability is reminiscent of March in "The Fox." This is Lawrence's description of March: "When she was out and about, in her puttees and breeches, her belted coat and her loose cap, she looked almost like some graceful, loose-balanced young man, for her shoulders were straight, and her movements easy and confident, even tinged with a little indifference, or irony." In his presentation of Elisa, Steinbeck's imagery is strikingly similar:

> She was thirty-five. Her face was lean and strong and her eyes were as clear as water. Her figure looked blocked and heavy in her gardening costume, a man's black hat pulled low over her eyes, clod-hopper shoes, a figured print dress almost completely covered by a big corduroy apron with four big pockets . . . her work with the scissors was over-eager, over-powerful. The chrysanthemum stems seemed too small and easy for her energy.

Of course it is mere speculation whether, or to what extent, Steinbeck was influenced by one or another of Lawrence's "masculine" women. What the women do share, and importantly so, is an intense strength of personality which sets them apart from so many of their retiring sisters in the literature of the twenties and thirties.

Elisa is essentially different from March, however, in the frustration she feels in her role as a rancher's wife; and part of Elisa's sense of frustration stems from the fact that her work, even the dirty work of gardening, remains "woman's work." When we first meet her she is tending the flower bed and watching her husband Henry discussing business with two men. "The three of them stood by the tractor shed, each man with one foot on the side of the little Fordson. They smoked cigarettes and studied the machine as they talked." Theirs is a sphere of money, tobacco, and machines from which she is deliberately excluded, although their conversation concerns the ranch and is therefore her affair as much as Henry's. Later, when Henry comes by to tell her about the transaction, he praises her for her gardening skills. "I wish you'd work out in the orchard and raise some apples that big," he comments; and she replies as to a challenge: "Maybe I could do it, too. I've got a gift with things, all right." But Henry obviously takes neither his remark nor her response seriously, for he says: "Well, it sure works with flowers." The fact that she strongly believes in her ability to perform paid work emerges again in her conversation with the itinerant pot-mender who boasts of his skill in the trade. She responds to this with a more positive challenge: "You might be surprised to have a rival some time. I can sharpen scissors, too. And I can beat the dents out of little pots. I could show you what a woman might do." But he tells her that his life, which she views romantically, "ain't the right kind of life for a woman."

Elisa may know nothing of the world beyond her valley, but she believes in her talents and in the possibility of a life more rewarding than her own. As the man and his equipage move on down the road, she stands at the fence watching him: "Her lips moved silently, forming the words 'Good-bye—good-bye.' Then she whispered, 'That's a bright direction. There's a glowing there.' " At the conclusion, when the man's disregard for her and her work has been revealed by his callous disposal of her gift of the plants, she grasps at adventure on a smaller scale: wine with dinner. She acknowledges the fact that a man's freedom is denied her by agreeing with her husband that she would, after all, probably dislike the prizefights, saying: "It will be enough if we can have wine. It will be plenty."

Elisa's ambiguous combination of traditionally masculine and feminine traits, more apparent than Mary Teller's, has a great deal to do with making her a plausible character. It is also fully half the concern of the story. The second major theme of "The Chrysanthemums" is related to the first in its revelation of Elisa's sensuality and the apparent sexual frustration she experiences in her marriage. While she and her husband appear to be friends, there is a definite failure of communication between them in the exchange of ideas; therefore, it is reasonable to assume a similar malfunction of sexual communication. The exchange of dialogue following her meeting with the tinker and prior to the couple's evening in town is a typical example of Henry's capacity for understatement and his embarrassment in her presence. Elisa has just dressed in the garment "which was the symbol of her prettiness" and is waiting on the porch for Henry to appear. As he emerges from the house,

> Elisa stiffened and her face grew tight. Henry stopped short and looked at her. "Why—why, Elisa. You look so nice!"
> "Nice? You think I look nice? What do you mean by 'nice?' "
> Henry blundered on. "I don't know. I mean you look different, strong and happy."
> "I am strong? Yes, strong. What do you mean 'strong?' "
> He looked bewildered. "You're playing some kind of a game," he said helplessly. "It's a kind of a play."

In the tinker, though, Elisa finds a man whose strength seems to match hers, although she later discovers his emotional poverty. Their brief encounter reveals an aspect of Elisa which is not seen in her dealings with Henry—her erotic potential.

At first, she reacts to the tinker with firm sales resistance but is brought into sympathy with him by the interest he expresses in her flowers. At last he shatters her resistance by asking for a pot of the young shoots to give a customer of his who has no chrysanthemums. It is at this point that Elisa begins to respond to him in a sexual fashion and shifts rapidly into the feminine, passive role. Steinbeck's imagery builds to Elisa's orgasmic speech to the tinker, then recedes in the afterglow of her bathing.

The first sign of change in Elisa is her desire to appear womanly for the man: "She tore off the battered hat and shook out her dark pretty hair." As she eagerly begins the transplanting, her gloves are discarded and she feels the rich earth between her bare fingers, an obviously sensual image. In the process she finds herself "kneeling on the ground looking up at him. Her breast swelled passionately." She is now below him in the traditional female position for intercourse. "Elisa's voice grew husky" as she tried to express for them both the feeling one has, alone, at night, beneath the stars:

> "Why, you rise up and up! Every pointed star gets driven into your body. It's like that. Hot and sharp and—lovely."

> Kneeling there, her hand went out toward his legs in the greasy black trousers. Her hesitant fingers almost touched the cloth. Then her hand dropped to the ground. She crouched low like a fawning dog.

Elisa is subconsciously contrasting him with her husband as a potential sexual partner. Ray B. West, Jr. says in *The Short Story in America, 1900–1950* (1952) that Elisa's vigorous bathing, following the tinker's departure, is an attempt on her part to maintain the physical vitality which he had aroused. It is equally probable that Elisa is attempting to wash away the taint of her own sensual approach to a stranger, whether or not he recognized her passion. The very idea that she might, even for a moment, have contemplated disloyalty toward the kind, if obtuse, Henry would impel her to scrub "legs and thighs, loins and chest and arms, until her skin was scratched and red." Steinbeck enumerates these parts of her body, the sexual ones, omitting mention of her face and hands which he had previously described as dirt-smudged. It is clear that he means this passage to be part of the story's sexual focus, and that he uses it as another detail which shows Elisa to be sexually repressed.

Despite whatever guilt Elisa feels as a result of the afternoon's experience, she also feels renewed confidence in her spiritual strength and in her physical attractiveness. Following the bath, she lingers awhile before the mirror appraising her body from different angles. Then she dresses slowly, luxuriously in her finest, newest clothing and expends a considerable amount of effort on her makeup.

Possibly because Elisa identifies so strongly with the male, at least in terms of a desire for adventure, she is vulnerable to the sexual appeal of a man. For whatever reasons, her husband does not stimulate her latent eroticism, so she has indulged herself in a fantasy involving a stranger. Her fantasy, however, is cruelly shattered by the tinker's deceit. She had believed they shared common emotions, that they actually communicated, but now she sees his talk as the salesman's trick that it was. In fact, he hadn't even the sensitivity to dump the plants furtively; he was too greedy to retain the pot. So she must see her small and broken flowers in the highway, a symbol of her broken dreams. Intuitively, she knows that her life will not change substantially, that the seasons will follow each other inexorably, and that only the birds will be migratory. Steinbeck says: "She turned up her coat collar so he [Henry] could not see that she was crying weakly—like an old woman." Indeed, part of the vision she must be seeing is herself as an old woman. Her dream of something in life beyond mere existence is crushed at this moment.

Henry is unaware of Elisa's suffering, nor could he offer effective consolation were he to notice her change of mood. Like the Tellers, the Allens are separated from one another by sexual, temperamental, and intellectual differences which they seem incapable of bridging. The women have certain needs of the spirit, the abstract nature of which keeps happiness forever elusive. The men are more practical, with greater involvement in physical concerns; but confronted by women whose malaise is partially due to a confusion of sexual identity, the men retreat from the masculine role of leadership, leaving the women to flounder between aggression and submission. Undoubtedly, part of the attraction the tinker holds for Elisa is his independence and the confidence of his manner which her husband apparently lacks. Likewise, Harry Teller, in his indulgence of Mary's whims, encourages her selfish dictation of their lives to the detriment of both partners. Steinbeck is not advocating that wives be submissive to their husbands; if his opinion on male-female relations can be interpreted at all from the two stories, it would seem to support a sharing of interests determined through real communication between people, so that none can say with Harry Teller: "Oh, Lord, I'm so lonely."

JACKSON J. BENSON

John Steinbeck: Novelist as Scientist

The fiction of John Steinbeck has had a special appeal to the scientist, for of all the major American writers of fiction in this century, Steinbeck alone has had an abiding interest in natural science and brought that interest to his writing. The marine scientist, in particular, has claimed Steinbeck for his own because of the writer's life-long attachment to the seashore and its animals. He was, according to several professional scientists who knew him, "a very good amateur biologist." Furthermore, if Steinbeck does have a claim on the attention of future generations of readers, much of that claim will be based on his concern with science, since he alone, among American novelists of his time, saw man as part of an ecological whole.

At the same time, however, Steinbeck's scientific outlook created many problems for him as an artist and contributed significantly to a generally negative response to much of his work by literary critics. His use of science put him in a position of isolation—often the critics did not understand what he was doing. Further, his use of ideas associated with science brought him into conflict with the novel form and its traditions, leading him into difficulties with characterization, plot, and point of view which he was only partially able to overcome. While the modern novel as a whole has tended to drift back toward the poetic and mythic, Steinbeck's fiction, particularly during those years when he was most heavily influenced by his

From *Novel: A Forum on Fiction* 10, no. 3 (Spring 1977). © 1977 by Novel Corporation.

marine biologist friend, Edward F. Ricketts, was often infused with large doses of naturalistic philosophy. Thus, his example not only provides some interest as an exception to the general flow of modern American fiction, it throws into sharp relief the central scientific-poetic duality of the novel form itself.

The novel form has always been attached to "science," in the broadest sense of the word. The English novel was born out of the Reformation, the middle-class version of the medieval romance. Its development and popularity must be linked in part to a change in the climate of belief. Largely by accident of inheritance and by an evolutionary adaptation, the novel, among all the literary species, assumed those characteristics which best fitted it to carry the burden of the major philosophical conflict of the post-Renaissance Western world: science versus religion, or the new faith versus the old. Neither poetry nor drama could adequately carry the burden of this conflict because each was already committed by origin and development to the old. It became the task of an essentially new form to explore the nature of reality, an ancient question brought into the center of modern consciousness by the power of science at last to command a degree of belief which roughly matched the power of religion.

I should add immediately that what I mean by "religion," for the purposes of the rather broad distinctions I am trying to draw here, is the whole spectrum of intuitive knowledge and the systems of belief derived from such intuition. I would include not only religion proper, but myth, poetic intuition, and even humanism, in so far as humanism develops a faith in man, his nature and destiny, based on intuition. The inclusion of humanism here, although awkward, is important, for much modern literature while not ultimately religious in a traditional sense, advocates the importance of man within a context which is religious in tone, material, and general attitude.

I do not think that the task of exploring the nature of reality was as much consciously pursued by the early novelists as it was thrust upon them by the nature of their form. Belief was essential, for the novels were written largely by those who earned their living by writing them, and they instinctively found that enjoyment of their fiction was linked in large measure to their ability to create a world in which the reader could believe and therefore participate. Fiction, as poetic imagination, mixed with fact or disguised as "factual" was basic to the early evolution of the form, and this mixture in turn created a medium which was by its very nature rent asunder by a profound philosophical dualism.

As Ian Watt and others have pointed out in some detail, the modern version of the long fictional narrative began with the "novel proper," the early writers often choosing such nonfiction forms as the letter, the diary, and the journal to lend credibility to their fictions. The very fact, of course, that writers such as Defoe and Richardson used these disguises so effectively (it did not matter that the audience might suspect a disguise—the impact of the form itself was enough to encourage credibility) is testimony to a changing climate of belief. The seeds of a philosophical dualism had been planted from the very beginning, however, for the published "journal" of Robinson Crusoe traces the fantastic adventures of an extraordinary man made ordinary through the description of the daily routine of a ship-wrecked sailor with a shopkeeper's mentality.

Of Steinbeck's predecessors in the American novel caught up in this dualism, Herman Melville presents a dramatic example. His awareness of the split is manifested most directly in the masterpiece of his mid-career, *Moby-Dick*. For in this novel, much to the consternation of its early readers, two versions of reality are presented side by side: a scientific catalogue of ordinary whales and a religious allegory of an extraordinary whale. Prior to *Moby-Dick,* Melville wrote fiction essentially drawn from the close observation which came out of personal experience with sailing ships and the sea; following *Moby-Dick,* his work became increasingly allegorical and in some instances obscure. It is important to note in this context that Melville viewed his early work with some contempt as superficial, and that his ultimate concern became a search for a satisfactory metaphysic. His choice would seem to be typical of many serious novelists: involved, perhaps inadvertently, in a dualism of tradition, form, and thought, the American writer of fiction seems to drift, sooner or later, toward the magnetism of the poetic-religious. The biographies of modern American novelists suggest that children do not grow up to be writers of fiction because they are interested in science, but rather perhaps because they are readers entranced with the world of adventure and romance that books offer to them. (Thomas Pynchon comes to mind as a possible exception to this rule.) They become conditioned toward speculation rather than investigation, and they become fascinated by the unknown rather than by the knowable.

Jack London, an immediate predecessor, and a novelist whose work Steinbeck in his own teens had read, serves as an example of the writer drawn into writing by his love of adventure. His life was devoted to a search for adventure and his experiences brought him a sharp apprehension of reality in opposition to his romantic dreams. In his well-known story "To Build a Fire," the two directions so typical of the modern American writer are brought together. The story suggests that the man who does not understand his place in nature and who has been betrayed by the rosey, comforting illusions of a civilization which has insulated him from the facts of the natural world, will die when he confronts the full power of a nature indifferent to his needs. The story becomes an ecological parable within the envelope of the adventure story, combining, as Steinbeck would in much of his fiction, dispassionate observation, human illusion, allegory, and a mystical personification of the forces of nature. The central impact of the story is to show man, self-deluded, at the mercy of a natural world he hardly understands—ironically the man's dog lives and adapts, while his master perishes.

One can approach the split we have been discussing from a formal point of view, as Northrop Frye and others have done, and think of it as a manifestation of a conflict between narrative traditions. Some time ago, Richard Chase in *The American Novel and Its Tradition* posited that the long fictional narrative can be divided, roughly, into two kinds: the novel, which tends to observe specific social relationships and activities more or less realistically, and the romance, which veers toward the "mythic, allegorical and symbolic forms." The influence of science, however, can be perceived only dimly in the background of such a generalized distinction. Inevitably the rise of science has extended the penetration and range of factual observation expressed in the novel considered as a whole. But the use of this range is not inevitable—realism remains only one among many possible directions for the novelist. And even when a realistic approach is employed by the novelist, it does not in itself demonstrate a devotion to, nor even consciousness of science.

Far more significant than form or method for determining the explicit impact of science on fiction is the discovery of underlying philosophy. The deliberate use of science, the conscious application of scientific thought to character and action, has been labeled "Naturalism." The novelist not only chooses to see man as physical and as a product of his environment, he usually goes out of his way to refute the traditional religious-mythic views of man's nature and destiny. His most typical theme is the irony of man's position in the modern world—clinging to old beliefs and forms, he is blind to reality and is victimized and even destroyed by the real nature of his environment. Precisely the point of the London story.

The novelist who espouses a scientific philosophy is caught in a trap, however. Narrative is in itself based on the old philosophy, on the assumptions that man can act, that he has a measure of free will, and that the choices he makes are made from genuine alternatives. These assumptions really define the nature of the traditional "story." By contrast, the purely naturalistic story would be, if one had access to all the data, something like a computer printout. Thus, the writer who tries to use a scientific point of view must be drawn into a split or conflict between the philosophy inherent in his form and the philosophy he brings to that form. When we look at the American naturalists at the turn of the century, we find that few of them were able to maintain a thorough-going naturalism in their writing. Within the framework of naturalistic fiction by such writers as Norris, Garland, London, Dreiser, and Crane, perhaps the purest work of this kind was a short story by Stephen Crane, "The Open Boat." In this work there are no choices. This is not a story of action, but a story of realization. While the essence of the traditional story is morality (action can be taken and judged in a religious or humanistic context), the essence of naturalistic fiction is perception.

"The Open Boat" focuses on that ironic perception basic to all naturalistic fiction—that the old values of a man-centered universe are revealed through experience to be false. After severe exposure to the ravages of the sea in an open boat, taking his turns at the oars day and night with little water and no food, the story's central character, the correspondent, comes to a realization of the irony and injustice of his situation. That his situation is unjust can only be maintained within the anthropocentric picture sustained by the Judeo-Christian tradition. The correspondent first asks, "Why?":

> If I am going to be drowned—if I am going to be drowned—if I am going to be drowned, why, in the name of the seven mad gods who rule the sea, was I allowed to come thus far and contemplate sand and trees?

He thinks of his suffering as a personal punishment, searches for cause and effect, and determines that his punishment has been wrongly administered, when, in fact, he has been betrayed by an inaccurate, poetic-religious map of reality:

> When it occurs to a man that nature does not regard him as important, and that she feels she would not maim the universe by disposing of him, he at first wishes to throw bricks at the temple, and he hates deeply the fact that there are no bricks and no temples. Any visible expression of nature would surely be pelleted with his jeers.

Later in the story the correspondent becomes aware that his situation cannot be approached from the question "Why?"—it is irrelevant. The only

thing relevant is that which "is," and the only relevant questions are
"*What* is the situation?" and "*How* can I deal with it?" The correspondent
comes to understand that nature was not cruel, nor "beneficient, nor
treacherous, nor wise. But she was indifferent, flatly indifferent." This
realization might be called, using the terminology from the Ed Ricketts-
John Steinbeck vocabulary, the moment of "non-teleological breakthrough."
It is the trauma of rejecting the religious world-view and adopting a
scientific world-view. However, such a nearly "pure" work of naturalism,
as this story, has been the exception. Most naturalists, particularly when
using the novel form, have struggled with the problems of the dualism we
have noted above, and their struggles have often led to deeply flawed
narratives.

In addition to the conflict with his form, the novelist who would bring
a scientific philosophy to his work faces other obstacles. Depending on
how heavily he attempts to press his perspective, he is in danger of being
cut off from literary tradition as a whole and from the modes of communication, such as allusion and symbol, which have evolved in that tradition.
(Connected to this problem is the conviction held by many in our time that
for narrative to be truly art, it must be essentially poetic and intuitive.) In
order to deal with this obstacle, the naturalist has tended to substitute the
use of image, and image combined with metaphor, for cultural symbol.
But this substitution has often led critics to attack such fiction on the basis
that it lacks significance. A case in point is the work of Ernest Hemingway.
Essentially a philosophical naturalist throughout much of his career, he
depended heavily on the techniques of image and irony. He was criticized
severely and repeatedly for lack of aesthetic dimension in his work. Whether
he unconsciously capitulated to this criticism in his late years or, like
Melville, was drawn in the end toward the religious-poetic by conviction is
not clear. In any case, with *The Old Man and the Sea* he produced a
semi-religious allegory, larded with mythic overtones, cultural symbols,
and nature romanticism.

If we are to examine Steinbeck's role as scientist, or any twentieth-
century American novelist's relationship to science, we must do so within
the context of the traditions and patterns we have just reviewed: the
dualism at the heart of prose fiction and the duality of the writer's own
experience as a result of his having encountered reality in a culture which
has endorsed an essentially poetic-religious view of life. Steinbeck was
born and reared a romantic, wrote his first novels as a romantic, and
maintained certain poetic-religious-mythic schemes of thought and feeling
throughout his lifetime. At the same time, he adopted certain attitudes and

approaches, as expressed in his fiction, which brought him closer to a scientific perspective than any other important modern American writer. The conflict of his early conditioning and the interest in science he acquired as an adult produced a particularly intense conflict within the schemes of the tradition which we have summarized. Furthermore, in so far as Steinbeck not only took a nonteleological view of reality, but went beyond that breakthrough to see a different kind of order, a physical order with certain moral and social imperatives, to that extent he was a writer who became something more than a traditional naturalist.

When I say he was born a romantic, I mean that his roots were in the adventure of the journey West to California taken by both his paternal and maternal grandparents. When he was young, a sister read the Greek myths to him, and from uncles, aunts, and parents he heard the Bible, Shakespeare, *Paradise Lost, Pilgrim's Progress,* and the fairy tales of Hans Christian Andersen. There was a split in the foundations of his imagination as produced by his early experiences with literature: on the one hand, there was deep attachment to what we have called here "romance"—to the fantastic, the magical, and the adventurous; on the other hand, there was a deeply ingrained feeling for the harsh judgments and dark imagery of fundamental religion. All in all, Steinbeck had been carefully nourished in a climate which was thoroughly unscientific in its approach to life. His mother, as Steinbeck once remarked, possessed a theology which "was a curious mixture of Irish fairies and an Old Testament Jehovah whom in her later life she confused with her father."

The early development of Steinbeck's talent reflected the climate within which it had been nourished. As a young teenager he wrote poems and gave them as presents to relatives, and by the time he was a junior in high school at the age of sixteen, he had decided to become a writer—a writer of the kind of tales of adventure which had excited him as a reader: Alexandre Dumas, Sir Walter Scott, Robert Louis Stevenson, and Jack London. At the age of seventeen, he went to Stanford, not that he thought university studies would help him toward his goal of becoming a writer, but to please his parents. But in his sophomore year, he became so restless that he decided, in Jack London fashion, to run off to sea. He left a note for a startled roommate that he was on his way to China. He was never able to get a ship, however, and stayed in San Francisco for a time, attempting to live the Bohemian life he thought a struggling young writer should, and then returned to Stanford.

Brief stays at college alternated with various jobs. Then he finally did sail aboard a freighter, but for New York, rather than China. He tried to further his apprenticeship by becoming a cub reporter in the big city. But he failed as a newspaperman (one story is that he could not report what he observed—he had to embellish everything he wrote with poetic flourishes), and returned to California to spend most of the next three and a half years in the Lake Tahoe area. During his twenties, Steinbeck's reading ranged widely from the Greek and Roman classics, to Dostoyevski and Zane Grey; but the writers that seem to have made the greatest impression on him were the romancers, popular at that time, James Branch Cabell and Donn Burne. While at Tahoe, Steinbeck spent most of his time, winter and summer, working on a series of novel manuscripts. Two of these, both romances, were published—*Cup of Gold* and *To a God Unknown*. Both were mythic and allegorical, as well as extremely poetic in execution.

Needless to say, there is very little in all this to suggest that Steinbeck had much interest in science. He did have a job as a bench chemist at the Spreckles Sugar factory near Salinas performing a perfunctory test on the distillate. He also worked on several occasions as a helper at trout hatcheries on Lake Tahoe. He did take a course in general zoology at Hopkins Marine Station one summer while going to Stanford. But none of this small connection with science had any relationship with his writing, writing which was generated essentially out of his reading and his imagination. Then two things happened at nearly the same time, and I think they are, in terms of Steinbeck's work during the nineteen thirties, of nearly equal importance. He married Carol Hennings and he met the marine biologist Ed Ricketts. Each drew Steinbeck out of his penchant for romance toward a more realistic fiction based on experience.

During the first two or three years of his marriage, while at the same time his friendship for Ricketts grew, Steinbeck appears to have experienced several "breakthroughs" in thought, and his direction as a writer changed markedly. One such breakthrough was his conversion to a social-political consciousness that he was willing to bring into his fiction. He had already experienced the disillusionment with the middle-class, Victorian view of life which has so often led modern American writers into realism. But it took the visible suffering produced by the depression, as well as the political consciousness of his wife and a new set of friends in the Monterey-Pacific Grove area, to displace his attraction for romance with a concern for observing life as it actually was. *In Dubious Battle,* published in 1936, shows the combined influences of Ricket's holistic, nonteleological philosophy—"observing things as they are in order to get an understanding of the whole"—and of Carol Steinbeck's social consciousness and preference for tough, realistic prose.

A second breakthrough came in terms of a new sense of his art as dependent on direct experience—not necessarily his own, but experience nevertheless. In this Steinbeck's wife was perhaps the most important influence. She was his severest critic and was intolerant of the lyrical prose style and the mystical-allegorical themes that her husband had labored to cultivate during the years prior to their marriage. She was very talented and perceptive and seemed to have a far better critical sense than her husband, realizing that if he continued to emulate Burne, his writing would continue to be second-rate. Going to his own experience, Steinbeck wrote several short stories and the short novels, *The Red Pony* and *Of Mice and Men,* during the early and mid-thirties. This fiction, along with *In Dubious Battle* (the material for which he got as second-hand experience from a strike organizer), is among Steinbeck's best and is far different in tone, style, and underlying philosophy from his early *Cup of Gold* and *To a God Unknown.*

A third change came during the early thirties in terms of what I have already described in discussing "The Open Boat" as a "non-teleological breakthrough," and it is here, in the adoption of this mode of thought, that Ed Ricketts no doubt played the most persuasive part. The foundations of Steinbeck's nonteleological thinking have been described rather fully in the recent book by Richard Astro, *John Steinbeck and Edward F. Ricketts: The Shaping of a Novelist,* and in Joel W. Hedgpeth's article, "Philosophy on Cannery Row," in Richard Astro and Tetsumaro Hayashi's *Steinbeck: The Man and His Work.* I can only point, first of all, to Ed Ricketts himself, whose thinking along these lines was initiated by his professor of marine biology at the University of Chicago, W. C. Allee; and, second, to the U.C.L.A. professor John Elof Boodin, whose organismic philosophy was brought to Steinbeck by Richard Albee, a long-time friend who joined the Steinbeck-Ricketts circle in the mid-thirties.

The resulting picture of the universe as derived from these sources and others, modified by much discussion and debate and by the personalities and backgrounds of Steinbeck and Ricketts, is too complex for a brief description. Let me simplify the picture by reminding the reader of two often quoted passages from *The Log from the Sea of Cortez:*

Non-teleological ideas derive through "is" thinking, associated with natural selection as Darwin seems to have understood it. They imply depth, fundamentalism, and clarity—seeing beyond traditional or personal projections. They consider events as outgrowths and expressions rather than results; conscious acceptance as a desideratum, and certainly as an all important prerequisite. Non-teleological thinking concerns itself primarily not with what should be, or could be, or might be, but rather with what actually "is"—attempting at most to answer the already sufficiently difficult questions *what* or *how,* instead of *why.*

and

Our own interest lay in relationships of animal to animal. If one observes in this relation sense, it seems apparent that species are only commas in a sentence, that each species is at once the point and the base of a pyramid, that all life is relational. . . . It is a strange thing that most of the feeling we call religious, most of the mystical outcrying which is one of the most prized and used and desired reactions of our species, is really the understanding and the attempt to say that man is related to the whole thing, related inextricably to all reality.

The passages above are really "Ricketts as interpreted by Steinbeck," since Ricketts's notes and essays were on the table where Steinbeck composed *The Log.* Nevertheless, he came to agree with the sentiments expressed in them long before *The Log* was written. The first significant expression of nonteleological and holistic thought is in *In Dubious Battle.* Doc Burton does not act so much as he looks to understand; what he wants to observe is men who, coming together as a group, assume the characteristics of an entirely different "individual." The expression of this thought continues in almost all of Steinbeck's fiction up through *East of Eden. The Red Pony* (parts of which were published before and after *In Dubious Battle*) uses Jody as an unwilling student of nature—his dreams of romance are reinforced with the optimism, the "personal projections" of Billy Buck. Buck is the false tutor—it is Jody's father, who is pictured so harshly, who really understands that nature's will must be done regardless of our feelings. What Jody must learn to accept is that the vultures are as much a part of nature as the pony.

The Darwinism of *The Red Pony* is brought from the conflict of animals to the conflict between men in *Of Mice and Men.* Originally titled "Something That Happened," we find again that the dreams of man, his personal projections, contradict the nature of reality. As engaging to our own sense of romance and sentiment as Lennie's and George's dream of a small ranch may be, the facts are that they do not have the power within the scheme of things to make that dream come true. Lennie kills without malice—animals and people die simply because of his strength. Lennie himself must die simply because within the society of man he is an anomaly and weak. The point in each case is that what happens, happens: things work themselves out as they must according to their nature.

In *The Grapes of Wrath* both personal projections (that little white house surrounded by orange trees in California) and traditional projections (religion, family, poetic justice) run afoul of the nature of human society as it actually is. Like Doc Burton of *In Dubious Battle*, Jim Casy can become an observer of things as they are only after he rejects his own personal projections and those of society's traditions as well. In a parody of Christ's religious purgation of the self, Casy goes into the wilderness to emerge with a scientific, nonteleological vision: "There ain't no sin and there ain't no virtue. There's just stuff people do. It's all part of the same thing." Along somewhat the same lines, the people in the various subcultures depicted in the comic novels—*Tortilla Flat, Cannery Row,* and *Sweet Thursday*—are able to achieve happiness in so far as they are able to deal with life on an "is" basis, rejecting both the personal and traditional projections typical of the larger society. Disaster strikes whenever individuals in the subculture are tempted to depart from their natural environment, their interdependent "tidepool" communities, to take on duties within the middle-class sea of values.

While Steinbeck's obvious sympathy for the subcultures irritated critics, his lack of sympathy and his stereotyping of characters in the microcosm of *The Wayward Bus* bothered them even more. The approach used in the comedies and in *The Wayward Bus* is roughly similar, but the observer in the comedies is on a "field trip," while the observer in *The Wayward Bus* has deliberately collected certain representative specimens in the field and put them together in a laboratory tank to observe their interreactions. Nevertheless, the topic of major concern in this novel is accepting what "is," just as it is also the topic of major concern in *East of Eden*.

Although the biblical materials in *East of Eden* may be more confusing than useful, if we can look beyond them (or see that Steinbeck is using religious materials to make a non-religious, philosophical point), we can perceive that the primary movement in the work is toward freedom—freedom from destructive illusion and self-delusion. At the end of the novel, as Adam Trask is dying, he is being reborn to a new perspective. Earlier, he could not see his wife for what she was because of his romantic projections, and then he could not see his sons because of a religious reaction which replaced his romanticism. Now, at last, he gains an opportunity to see things as they are when he realizes that man is not bound by the scheme of sin and virtue, that man is free to be, and in being, he is what he is. By freeing himself, Trask is able to bless and free his son.

These patterns which express a nonteleological point of view, in one way or another, can be seen as having some similarities to the realistic-naturalistic fiction of the late nineteenth and early twentieth centuries. Yet, there is at least one important difference. In realism-naturalism, one sees and therefore rejects traditional or personal projections. One would like to believe, but in light of the evidence, one cannot. The resulting disillusionment, as in the case of the correspondent in "The Open Boat," often leads the individual to the anger of someone who has been swindled. By contrast, if the individual fully assumes a nonteleological point of view, he rejects traditional and personal projections so that he *can* see. The fiction of such writers as Crane, Norris, and Dreiser often suggests that the dream is better than the reality, but the dream is impossible to hold onto. This pattern does appear to some degree in Steinbeck's fiction when the nonteleological perspective is applied outside the novel or story by the author (in assumed conjunction with the reader). Both *Of Mice and Men* and *The Red Pony* move toward this perspective—they can be read as novels of disillusionment. But when a nonteleological point of view is established within the work of fiction itself, as it is in *In Dubious Battle* and *The Grapes of Wrath*, the resulting emotional tone is far different. As nonteleological observers within their respective novels, Doc Burton and Jim Casy are islands of calm within the strife and bitterness which surround them. It is significant that several of these characters are called "Doc" (and patterned in some degree after Steinbeck's real-life scientist friend, Ed Ricketts) in that their main characteristic is a scientific detachment. This is even true of Jim Casy whose "other-worldliness" is ironically more like the dispassionate, determined scientist than the Christ figure he has so often been compared to.

The contrast between the nonteleological observer and the characters around him who are caught up in illusion brings a somewhat new dimension to the basic realistic-romantic dualism of the novel of which we have spoken. The actions of the strikers in *In Dubious Battle*, of the bulk of the migrants in *The Grapes of Wrath*, of Mack and the Boys in *Cannery Row*, and of the Trask family (including Cathy) in *East of Eden* are as futile and unseeing as those of rats trapped in a maze. From a tragic point of view, this is mankind hopelessly captured by the myths of the past and personal predilections which make it impossible for man to rise above the maze to see it as a whole and therefore escape. From a comic point of view in Steinbeck's ostensibly "light" fiction, this is the Keystone Cops all running into each other and falling over themselves while Doc goes quietly about his business and, resigned to the foolishness of men, tries to pick up the pieces.

The dualism in the comedies—*Cannery Row* and *Sweet Thursday*—leads to humor in that the contrast is weakened and the illusions are foolish rather than serious. The contrast is weakened in that Mack and the Boys are in themselves somewhat more nonteleologically directed than society as a whole. As bums, or rather as successful bums (who know how to manage other people's illusions to their own benefit), they have already been disillusioned by society's myths, and being outside society, they too are usually observers. Thus, they are not so very different from Doc, the prime observer. The trouble starts when they depart from their disillusionment and their roles as observers. But the trouble is comic—minor and short-lived. It is all, including Doc's romantic departure into the sunset, riding his "bucking" car with the reformed saloon girl, palpable nonsense, a parody of sentimentality. The first book of the series, *Cannery Row*, begins with a look at life through a peephole and the parting gift of Mack and the Boys to Doc at the end of *Sweet Thursday* is a telescope.

Seeing and not-seeing, reality and self-delusion, these are the materials that Steinbeck plays with, sometimes seriously, sometimes humorously. To some degree it is the same game that novelists, from Sterne to Nabokov, have always played with the reader. But for many novelists, the discovery of reality has been a matter of regret, a sad necessity. For Steinbeck the emphasis is reversed. At that point when nonteleological thinking enters Steinbeck's work, man is seen as part of the natural world—what is sad is that man refuses to recognize that he is a part of nature. The novel tradition still clings to the belief that although man's dreams, his myths and his poetry, may lead him astray, they also separate him from and raise him above nature. While Steinbeck recognizes that man is different, he proposes that his differentness—namely, his ability to see beyond his own immediate needs and to understand his place in the picture of nature as a whole—should make him a better member of the natural community. At the core of disillusionment, as we find it in such naturalistic novels as Dreiser's *Sister Carrie*, Norris's *The Octopus*, London's *Martin Eden*, Hemingway's *The Sun Also Rises*, or Fitzgerald's *The Great Gatsby*, there is an inescapable melancholy and nostalgia. At the core of Steinbeck's best work, there is anti-sentimentality that is almost unbearable—the blind futility of strikers and employers in *In Dubious Battle*, the cold inevitability of the vulture in *The Red Pony,* the hunt for Lennie in *Of Mice and Men,* and the anti-poetry of the starving old man at Rose of Sharon's breast in the ending of *The Grapes of Wrath.*

Although I think charges of sentimentality against Steinbeck's fiction have often been glibly applied and usually overstated (there is much in the surface manner which is sentimental, and much more which appears to be, but which is not), that is not to say that his fiction does not have serious weaknesses and inconsistencies. Many of his difficulties can be traced directly to his efforts to employ a nonteleological vision as a basis for his form and technique. The source of these difficulties becomes clear when we realize that the nonteleological position expressed in the passages from *The Log,* as quoted above, contradicts rather sharply many of the basic attitudes expressed in and through the traditional forms of fictional narrative.

Since fictional narrative is essentially focused on conflict—man in conflict with other men and/or his environment—it suggests a world of cause and effect (contrary to the nonteleological view), of difficulty and remedy, and it implies, further, a separation of man from man and from his environment (contrary to the proposition that man is part of the "whole picture"). It is true that the scientist sees the natural world in continuous conflict. But if he is a pure scientist (not looking for ways to kill mosquitoes), he does not take sides. Fiction, on the other hand, almost always involves "side-taking." For conflict, as the essence of plot, attaches values to one side or the other as a matter of course.

Furthermore, the very way a story is told—the technical point of view—attaches, in itself, a set of values to the story content. Whereas the concept of plot suggests the overlaying of a set of values (from religion, cultural myth or attitude, or whatever) onto a series of events, point of view usually suggests that reality is indeed essentially a matter of personal projection. Whereas plot imposes ethnocentricity, point of view imposes egocentricity.

And, again, characterization runs into similar difficulties when it encounters the nonteleological formulation. As just noted in regard to point of view, the more personalized the narration, the more egocentric the focus, so that the narrator, as a character in fiction, imposes a teleology on events. As expressions of conflict, the protagonist and antagonist project a traditional value system (particularly if they can be seen as hero and villain). Indeed, in the very act of making a character "sympathetic" or "human," an author imposes a value system on his material.

Thus, the essential ingredients of fiction all come into conflict, to some degree, with the nonteleological position. Can a novelist hold a nonteleological position about the nature of reality and still function as a novelist? The answer illustrated by Steinbeck must be, I should think, yes: he can function, but he will be rather constantly forced into a position of contradiction and compromise. Furthermore, he will inevitably come into conflict with his form, altering it or perverting it, depending on the perspective with which his changes are viewed, and he must offend, to some extent, the preconceptions, or "standards" of his readers. The nonteleological position tends to restrict Steinbeck's use of various storytelling devices. To be consistent with his philosophy, he must, as a general rule, tell his story as impersonally as possible. Since the first person point of view is clearly the most egocentric, Steinbeck, during his "non-teleological period," does not use it. (His only major use of the first person is in his final novel, *The Winter of Our Discontent.*) Instead, Steinbeck uses the third-person omniscient point of view and, in the novels written as plays, the dramatic third person. The third-person omniscient point of view is that which best presents an overview of the interaction between characters. Steinbeck favors what might be called a "community overview" wherein he stands above a group of people, and using this picture of the whole as a reference point, he focuses on one character or incident after another, returning usually to place the individual scene within the larger context.

One of the marks of Steinbeck's work is this sequential focus on a variety of characters and scenes; we find it in his novels from the early *The Pastures of Heaven* to the late *East of Eden.* And because of this serial focus, what might normally be called minor characters and events receive, generally, more attention than they do in the work of other writers who use a more personalized point of view, organizing their fiction around the evolving purposes and thoughts of a single character. But because Steinbeck's view is often so diffuse, his work is usually in danger of losing unity, power, and direction. Furthermore, there can be, as in *The Wayward Bus,* an impersonality which, although appropriate to the nonteleological position, may alienate the reader's affections.

Plot can also be weakened by the impersonal, sequential focus. Suspense is dissipated by the lack of personal involvement in the motivation and fate of a single character. The fate of the central character in a number of Steinbeck's novels evolves so impersonally and is so tied to the general situation, that we do not really care very much about what happens to him. This is our reaction, I suspect, to such characters as Mac in *In Dubious Battle,* to Danny in *Tortilla Flat,* or to Juan Chicoy in *The Wayward Bus*—if, indeed, we can even refer to these characters as "central" in the usual sense of the term. Actually, not only does Steinbeck's use of the impersonal point of view with a sequential focus tend to act against the development of a strong central character, but the nonteleological position itself stands in opposition to emphasis on any single character other than as a reference point (Tom Joad), a sample of a characteristic part of the whole (Mac in *In Dubious Battle*), or an unusual specimen or mutation (Lennie in *Of Mice and Men*). That is, the choice of a particular character for extended observation is guided by what could be called "scientific interest," rather than by traditional literary criteria as dictated by a mythic-romantic view of man. Thus, the protagonist-hero is out of bounds for Steinbeck, not only because of the mythic-romantic value system such a character presupposes, but because such a character can only function within a teleological framework of individual triumph or disaster. In *In Dubious Battle,* by contrast, Doc Burton observes that the strike leader, Mac, may be as much the product of the group functioning as a group, as a leader functioning as a cause behind group activity.

Contrary to the typical "side-taking" which focuses the author's favor on a single individual, the implied author's approval or disapproval in the Steinbeck novel is likely to be applied to the entire group or "colony" more or less evenly. We are led to like nearly everyone in *Cannery Row,* we tend to be indifferent to nearly all the characters in *In Dubious Battle,* and we find none of the characters in *The Wayward Bus* to be particularly likable. Since there is seldom anyone in his novels who can be labeled "hero" or "villain," Steinbeck has been accused of failing to make moral discriminations. Actually, since in Jim Casy's words "there ain't no sin and there ain't no virtue," Steinbeck tends to follow in Mark Twain's footsteps in condemning most not those who "sin," but those who make such moral judgments.

In an age in which our culture, and hence very often the novel, is concerned with the internal workings of man's mind, Steinbeck's fiction is notably exterior in its point of view. Of course, it must be if he is going to focus on what "is" as matter of what is observed, eschewing as much as possible special pleading. Occasionally through the omniscient narrator we do enter the mind of a character, but extended use of some kind of interior monologue is rare, and it is always filtered through the sensibility of the narrator. Strangely enough, the power of Steinbeck's fiction often comes from the fact that we *do not* have direct knowledge of his characters' thoughts. Instead, we often hear his characters struggling to express their thoughts and feelings aloud, and in that struggle what they think and feel gains an authenticity and power that might be lost in a more direct presentation.

Another technique, in addition to dialogue, by which Steinbeck presents states of mind consists in using an exterior landscape to represent the inner landscape. This technique is tied to Steinbeck's heavy dependence on scene to perform functions in his work which are most typically assigned to other fictional techniques, and it is appropriate in light of the fact that his characters are so often closely connected, in temperament and state of being, to their surroundings. What goes on inside Elisa Allen, in "The Chrysanthemums," is more perfectly represented in her flowers and her care for them than could be stated in her mind or by the narrator reading her mind. Most important, from a nonteleological standpoint, the way that men tend their gardens—as they often do literally in Steinbeck's fiction—is observable, whereas the inner workings of their minds are not. This is one area—depth of characterization—in which I do not think Steinbeck may be always as weak as some readers have assumed, for a paradox is involved here. Sometimes the outside is more truly indicative of inner condition than the inside, itself, laid bare. We feel that we know Elisa Allen almost as well as we know Mrs. Dalloway, even though Virginia Woolf has two hundred seventy-three more pages, most of which is Mrs. Dalloway's stream-of-consciousness, to reveal her to us.

Scene carries a further burden as well, in that it is often in Steinbeck's work the basic medium for plot development. With a few exceptions, plot in the usual sense of the term is not very important in his fiction. As we have already noted, normally developed, plot is essentially a teleological formulation—it traces causes and effects, dwells on motivation, and inevitably involves "side-taking" in respect to an evolving conflict. To avoid being enmeshed in traditional plot, Steinbeck seldom examines or emphasizes motive—the effect he strives for is the presentation of events as they evolve out of conditions, as things that "simply happen," while trying at the same time to remain neutral to his characters, or at least trying to treat most of them pretty much the same.

Instead of characters carrying us through a series of actions in particular locales, it is, frequently in Steinbeck's fiction, the locales which shift or move, carrying the characters, in a sense, along with the change in scene. The drama here is the drama of circumstances, rather than that of evolving character cognition. Purposeful action by characters is not abandoned entirely, of course, but it is usually made secondary to a narrative flow animated by the larger purpose of observation and examination. Revealing of this method of plot development are Steinbeck's notes for *The Grapes of Wrath* in which he talks of taking his characters across the mountains, having them travel to the town of Brawley, and bringing them into the government camp. Clearly, he is interested in what happens to people *within* a particular social-physical environment. Note that *The Grapes of Wrath* ends not with an event, a "plot development" or twist, but with a *scene*. This final scene is not a resolution of the conflict for the Joads. We know that they will be further hurt by their own and other men's illusions. The scene is rather a resolution for the reader, who has been taken in tow by the narrator to witness one set of conditions after another. It is almost as if we as readers had been shown a series of slides recording "that which happens" in this environment and that. The resolution, significantly, is one for the observer, rather than for the observed. No novel, it seems to me, could operate more in the spirit of science than this.

The rationale behind this fiction would seem to lie in the fact that scene most clearly and directly expresses the condition of what "is." Thus, plot moves from condition to condition, and the structure of Steinbeck's novels usually involves contrast and parallel of condition, almost musical in its contrapuntal patterning. Man is perceived as an intimate part of his environment; indeed, character can be often perceived as a function of scene. Within such a scientific perspective—and I think that is exactly what the emphasis on scene provides—man's role is diminished. Regardless of the sentiments expressed within the dramatic surface of Steinbeck's fiction, his scheme of values is ultimately anti-romantic and totally unsentimental. What so many readers cannot forgive him for is not that he has denied God, the more typical naturalist's sin, but that he has denied the importance of man.

Conflict in the Steinbeck novel usually arises out of the inability of man to function in harmony with his environment, social or physical (and the two are seen in Steinbeck's work as interdependent). Such a conflict brings us back once more to Steinbeck's peculiar use of the basic dualism of the novel form, as illusion blinds man to what he should see in order to act in harmony with others. The conflict can be resolved once man takes off the blinders of social myth (often, in Steinbeck, respectability) and romantic self-delusion (often manifested as some form of egotism, greed, or self-indulgence). The final scene of *The Grapes of Wrath* defines such a resolution rather precisely. An old man at a young girl's breast is totally unacceptable to middle-class respectability because the image is "nasty." Within a scientific perspective, however, such a reaction is nonsense. On a deeper level of objection, the scene violates our romantic-erotic imagery, a culturally imposed illusion, as well as our traditional religious imagery. Yet within the physical-social landscape as it actually exists at the end of the novel, the scene is totally natural and harmonious. That many have violently objected to the scene proves Steinbeck's point exactly.

Furthermore, that the scene pinpoints a moment of natural joy amidst the pathos of the natural disaster of the flood defines the difference between Steinbeck's nonteleological naturalism and that employed by the realists-naturalists at the turn of the century. In "The Open Boat" there is, as I have said, a nonteleological breakthrough, but it leads to a sense of emptiness and betrayal. The temple is found to have disappeared, and nothing is found to replace it. But here in the final scene of *The Grapes of Wrath*, there is a sense that man can survive *in* nature if he is, in turn, himself natural. That there can be comfort in the nonteleological realization does not, as a rule, occur to the realists-naturalists.

There is, in this connection, a calm acceptance at the heart of Steinbeck's best fiction which has not often been consciously recognized, although I believe that humanist readers have reacted with instinctive irritation to it. While acceptance was not a large part of the Steinbeck temperament, it became, possibly through the influence of Ricketts, part of his philosophy which made part of his writing discipline. Steinbeck privately fumed in response to the many social injustices of the 1930s, but he did not want to write novels which were social tracts, and he made a powerful effort to restrain his indignation and his instincts for satire. His first draft (if one can call it that, since it has little connection with the final product) of *The Grapes of Wrath* was a bitter satire called *L'Affaire Lettuceberg,* which Steinbeck's first wife described for me as a social and political cartoon of Salinas. (Although she did not remember the draft as being so, I suspect from the title that it was about the outrageous incidents surrounding the 1936 Salinas lettuce strike.) Although he had sixty-thousand words, Steinbeck burned the manuscript and went on to write a novel which he felt was more philosophical than social. On an immediate level, as demonstrated in *The Forgotten Village,* Steinbeck believed in progress as provided by scientific knowledge, but in the long view, the view which stands behind most of his work, he saw man in a larger scientific perspective as only a small part of a very large and complex pattern.

The most common complaint about Steinbeck's fiction has been, of course, that he deals with, or plays with, his characters as if they were puppets, creating characters who are stereotypes or who appear to function more as if they were animals than men. And such assessments are largely valid—he does see man as an animal, albeit a rather gifted animal. The real question, however, is whether such a view of man is, as implied, necessarily an artistic fault. Perhaps Steinbeck has been a less accomplished novelist as a result of his adherence to certain views which might be called "scientific," or it may be simply that there is a fundamental difference in philosophy between the critics and the author.

Much of the negative reaction to Steinbeck's characterization arises, I suspect, from the nonteleological prohibition of the heroic protagonist, a prohibition which runs counter to our cultural taste even in an age of literary anti-heroes. And Steinbeck's central characters are not quite anti-heroes, either. If they fail, their failure is not usually a failure to act, but a failure to see. In many of Steinbeck's novels a philosophical character with whom the author's essential sympathy lies is paired with a man of action. (Sometimes, as in the pairing of Jim Casy with Tom Joad in *The Grapes of Wrath* and Lee and Adam Trask in *East of Eden,* there is a tutor-tyro relationship similar to the one described by Earl Rovit in regard to Hemingway's fiction.) The philosophical character seldom acts, while the man of action does not usually act very effectively or very well. Mac in *In Dubious Battle,* Billy Buck in *The Red Pony,* Danny in *Tortilla Flat,* Tom Joad in *The Grapes of Wrath,* Mack in *Cannery Row,* Juan Chicoy in *The Wayward Bus,* George in *Of Mice and Men,* Adam Trask in *East of Eden*—each is the man of action who one way or another, one time or another, messes things up and is a parody of the traditional protagonist who overcomes obstacles to achieve a satisfactory resolution. Steinbeck's point is, of course, that you don't act to gain results—a teleological formulation—you *look* in order to *understand.*

The final scene in *East of Eden* exemplifies as metaphor the triumph of perception as against heroic action. Adam Trask, the central character, is throughout the novel the "man of action" who messes things up. He is not an anti-hero, nor is he the usual victim of circumstances one finds in naturalistic-realistic fiction. If he is victimized at all, it is as a result of his own stubborn lack of perception. At the end of the novel he is paralyzed—that is, he can no longer act. And at this moment he is finally able to understand. In setting up the antithesis between action and perception, Steinbeck, it seems to me, has in this sense also managed to bring the basic romantic-realistic duality of fiction into a new stage of evolution.

Unfortunately for Steinbeck, however, there is nothing very dynamic, in the traditional sense of what fiction does, in the processes of looking and understanding. The resulting penalty that he must pay is the danger of stagnation in his work: except for *The Grapes of Wrath,* where the changing scene and the journey motif provide a kind of dynamism, the long novels—*East of Eden* and *The Winter of Our Discontent*—are often boring. Steinbeck's worst fault as a novelist is not weak characterization or sentimentality, but stagnation. That he is so often static in his fiction without being dull is a tribute to a very skillful prose style and an ability to see things from unusual perspectives. A book like *Cannery Row* is a masterpiece of a kind—witty, original, and amusing, it carries the reader along by sheer force of the narrator's personality and unique way of looking at things. At the same time, almost nothing of any consequence at all happens in the novel. Steinbeck's greatest successes—*In Dubious Battle, Tortilla Flat, Of Mice and Men, The Grapes of Wrath,* and *Cannery Row*—are all triumphs of perception, so that his adoption of the nonteleological approach must be said to have had its advantages as well as its disadvantages. It provided that edge of differentness that every writer must have if his work is to make its mark and be remembered.

John Steinbeck's exact place in the history of the American novel and his contribution to the evolution of the novel form are yet to be determined. Too much prejudice is still attached to his life and too much confusion still surrounds his goals and methods for any kind of objective assessment to be made at this time. Nevertheless, when that assessment is made, I think those who make it will be bound to acknowledge that frequent use of scientific attitudes and methods in his fiction which took him beyond the tradition of naturalism-realism into an achievement purely his own. Perhaps no such thing as a novelist who is also a scientist is possible—a writer who consistently brings a thoroughgoing scientific philosophy and methodology to the writing of fiction. But John Steinbeck went further in this direction than any other modern American writer of distinction has, and as far, perhaps, as any writer can. His attempts led to some failures and some rather extraordinary successes. His work, in its own way, was often as experimental and daring as that of any number of other modern writers whom we honor for having extended the presumed limits of artistic expression.

JOHN J. CONDER

Steinbeck and Nature's Self:
The Grapes of Wrath

Both Dreiser and Dos Passos saw the self as a product of mechanisms and hence incapable of freedom, and both postulated the existence of a second self beyond the limitations of determinism. Dreiser arrived late at the notion and, borrowing it wholesale from Brahmanic thought, barely tested its meaning, save to see it as the source of man's freedom. Although Dos Passos never developed a version of such a self, he early found its existence and suppression the cause of man's misery and, in elaborating on that theme, he was able to enlarge a cluster of themes and attitudes associated with a second self—in particular those associated with its relationship to society and to nature. In *The Grapes of Wrath*, Steinbeck renders his version of a second self in man and brings to mature development that cluster of themes and attitudes. Significantly, he brings them to maturity within a framework of determinism and so harmonizes authentic freedom and determinism in a way that Dos Passos never could do, since the second self, the true source of man's freedom, remains forever an embryo in his pages.

The interchapters of Steinbeck's novel create a network of interlocking determinisms through their emphasis on the operations of abstract, impersonal forces in the lives of the Oklahomans. Chapter 5 is especially effective both in capturing the poignancy of the human situation created by such forces and in pointing to the kind of deterministic force underlying the others in the novel. In one fleeting episode a nameless Oklahoman who

From *Naturalism in American Fiction: The Classic Phase.* © 1984 by The University sity Press of Kentucky.

threatens the driver of a bulldozer leveling his house is told that armed
resistance is futile, for the driver acts in the service of the bank, and "the
bank gets orders from the East." The Oklahoman cries, "But where does it
stop? Who can we shoot?" "I don't know," the driver replies. "Maybe
there's nobody to shoot. Maybe the thing isn't men at all. Maybe . . . the
property's doing it." Or at least the Bank, the monster requiring "profits all
the time" in order to live and dwarfing in size and power even the owner
men, who feel "caught in something larger than themselves."

The vision that appears here has a name: economic determinism. This
view does not say that man has no free will. One might indeed find
among a group of bank presidents a corporate Thoreau who prefers jail
(or unemployment) to following the demands of the system. It merely
asserts that most men charged with the operation of an economic structure
will act according to rules requiring the bank's dispossession of its debtors
when a disaster renders them incapable of meeting payments on their
mortgaged property. Far from denying free will, such determinism fully
expects and provides for the willed resistance of the Oklahomans. The
police take care of that. Nor is this vision without its moral component,
though neither the police nor the owner men can be held individually
responsible. "Some of the owner men were kind," Steinbeck writes, "because they hated what they had to do, and some of them were angry
because they hated to be cruel, and some of them were cold because they
had long ago found that one could not be an owner unless one were cold."
These anonymous men are not devil figures but individuals performing
functions within a system, so the work indicts the system rather than
individuals who act in its service. In the case of the Oklahomans, the
indictment is founded on a fundamental irony: societies, designed to
protect men from nature's destructive features—here a drought—complete
nature's destructive work, expelling men from the dust bowl into which
nature's drought has temporarily transformed their farms.

But the expulsion of the Oklahomans is not the only inexorable
consequence of the operation of economic force. These men, women, and
children who "clustered like bugs near to shelter and to water" automati-
cally create in their camps a society within the larger society, acting according to the same instinctual dictate that initially made the Joad family,
seeking self-preservation, seem "a part of an organization of the unconscious." "Although no one told them," the families instinctively learned
"what rights are monstrous and must be destroyed"—the "rights" of rape,
adultery, and the like—and which must be preserved. Instinct welds the
group "to one thing, one unit"; and the contempt, fear, and hostility they

encounter as they traveled the highways "like ants and searched for work, for food" reinforce the bonds of group solidarity by releasing an anger whose ferment "changed them . . . united them" all the more. Here is the basis of that much-remarked-on shift in the novel from farmer to migrant, from "I" to "we," from family to group.

This emphasis upon the spontaneous development of a social group is not limited to the interchapters; but it is there that Steinbeck notes not only the inevitability of its development but, more important, the concurrent emergence of a group consciousness and the inevitable future consequences that its emergence entails. Economic determinism thus spawns responses that are biologically determined. Of course the scope of Steinbeck's biological determinism is sharply limited. He states with certainty but two simple facts: that the "anlage of movement" possessed by the oatbeards, foxtails, and clover burrs of chapter 3 has its counterpart in the anlage of "two squatting men" discussing their common plight, and that the realization of the potential in such anlage is inevitable. As the narrative voice proclaims to the owner men: "Here is the anlage of the thing you fear. This is the zygote. For here 'I lost my land' is changed; a cell is split and from its splitting grows the thing you hate—'*We* lost *our* land.' " Thus, forces that destroy one community create another by stimulating the communal anlage inherent in instinct, which sets the primary goals of life—in the Oklahomans' case, survival.

But in a novel that so beautifully portrays society as a system of interrelated forces, there is more to the matter than what has just been described. If economic determinism breeds biological determinism, biological determinism in turn spawns an inevitable social conflict that in time becomes an historically determined sequence of events with predictable outcome. Although there are references to it elsewhere, chapter 19 most clearly transforms this economic determinism into an historical one. It describes armed Californians, who earlier had stolen land from Mexicans, guarding the stolen land. Following the pattern of the Romans ("although they did not know it"), "they imported slaves, although they did not call them slaves: Chinese, Japanese, Mexicans, Filipinos." Later appear the dispossessed Oklahomans of the East, "like ants scurrying for work, for food, and most of all for land." When the slaves rebel, Steinbeck, using repetition, emphasizes the cause-effect relationship between the migrants' condition and their rebellion against it. "The great owners, striking at the immediate thing, the widening government, the growing labor unity; . . . not knowing these things are results, not causes. Results, not causes; results, not causes. The causes lie deep and simply." And that he believes

these causes compel the appearance of the effect proceeding from them—
that is, believes the causes determine that effect's emergence—becomes
clear in chapter 19 when he associates "the inevitability of the day" when
the owners must lose their land with their violent temporizing: "Only
means to destroy revolt were considered, while the causes of revolt went
on."

But now some observations about the relation of the interchapters
and the plot of *The Grapes of Wrath* are needed in order to show that
Steinbeck's determinism can embrace freedom of the will because his
literary structure creates a statistical determinism. The interchapters display the growth of a group consciousness controlled by instinct's response
to the dynamic of economic forces. This emphasis is carried into the story
in a variety of ways, most notably through Ma's insistence on keeping
the family together. But in the story proper, instinct does not rule
each person with equal power. The instinctual power that drives the
group in the interchapters is unequally distributed among its individual
members. Granpa's resistance to leaving Oklahoma testifies to the power
of age to overcome the instinct to survive. And age is not the only force
limiting the role of instinct in individual lives. Attached to his land, Muley
Graves refuses to leave it in order to depart for California. He makes a
choice that reduces him to "a ol' graveyard ghos' " living by night as a
trespasser on land once his own. Noah finds the hardships of the journey
greater than the comfort derived from the group and leaves, last seen
walking by a river into the greenery of the surrounding countryside to an
unknown future. Connie, angry that he did not remain to work for the
bank (and thus aid in the Oklahomans' dispossession), abandons his
pregnant wife Rosasharn.

In the plot, then, free will plays a major role. Even those who remain
with the group make numerous free choices to assure its survival, as Ma's
words about the need to get to California testify: "It ain't kin we? It's will
we?" This emphasis on choice and free will sets limits on the rule of
instinct, limits that avoid reducing the individual to the level of a will-less
animal, a mere pawn of instinct. Man's possessions of instincts roots him
in nature, but he is different from other things in nature, as Steinbeck
makes clear by describing in chapter 14 man's willingness to "die for a
concept" as the "one quality [that] is the foundation of Manself . . .
distinctive in the universe." And this emphasis on man's uniqueness in
nature, so inextricably related to his will, in turn limits the scope of the
novel's historical determinism, which is based on Steinbeck's biological
determinism. Even in the group that will give history its future shape, there

are individuals who will depart from the historical patterns which that group is aborning.

Seen in this way, Steinbeck's determinism does not at first sight seem a far cry from Dos Passos's, at least insofar as the economic base that underlies their respective deterministic outlooks issues in a statistical determinism for each writer. But Steinbeck's interchapters are a technical innovation that create a significant expansion and difference of vision, first appearances notwithstanding. Steinbeck gains two major advantages from them. First, by creating this preserve for rendering abstract social forces, he releases a considerable number of other chapters—his plot chapters—for portraying characters as developing states of consciousness rather than as those fragments of force which they seem to be in *Manhattan Transfer*. He thereby can *emphasize* the existence of free will in his novel. Just by making freely willed decisions the basis of his statistical determinism, in other words, he gives will a role more prominent than the one it plays in Dos Passos's work, where chance prevails and will is nugatory.

The second advantage is of far greater importance because it shows Steinbeck's idiosyncratic way of harmonizing determinism and freedom. In addition to portraying abstract forces operating on a grand scale in space and time, those chapters also are instrumental in showing the change in the group from an organism biologically determined by instinct and externally determined by social forces to an organism that achieves rationality and hence a freedom of will capable of transcending the bonds of determinism. The interchapters are indispensable because they dramatize Steinbeck's belief that a group is a living organism possessing a life of its own independent of the individuals who comprise it, and the implementation of that view is a part of the novel's genius.

Steinbeck clarifies his view of a group in *Sea of Cortez*, a collaboration of sorts, where in a passage specifically written by him he uses marine analogies to explain his sense of the normal relation of an individual to the group of which he is a part:

> There are colonies of pelagic tunicates which have taken a shape like the fingers of a glove. Each member of the colony is an individual animal, but the colony is another individual animal, not at all like the sum of its individuals. Some of the colonists, girdling the open end, have developed the ability, one against the other, of making a pulsing movement very like muscular action. Others of the colonists collect the food and distribute it, and the outside of the glove is hardened and

protected against contact. Here are two animals, and yet the same thing. . . . So a man of individualistic reason, if he must ask, "Which is the animal, the colony or the individual?" must abandon his particular kind of reason and say, "Why, it's two animals and they aren't alike any more than the cells of my body are like me. I am much more than the sum of my cells and, for all I know, they are much more than the division of me." There is no question in such acceptance, but rather the basis for a far deeper understanding of us and our world.

This quotation stresses the individuality of the group and the uniqueness, apart from it, of its component elements. In the following quotation Steinbeck introduces an added dimension in the larger animal, here a school of fish:

And this larger animal, the school, seems to have a nature and drive and ends of its own. . . . If we can think in this way, it will not seem so unbelievable . . . that it seems to be directed by a school intelligence. . . . We suspect that when the school is studied as an animal rather than as a sum of unit fish, it will be found that certain units are assigned special functions to perform; that weaker or slower units may even take their place as placating food for the predators for the sake of the security of the school as an animal.

Biology thus seems to confirm the eternal copresence of the one and the many. Applying the thrust of the thought of this passage to the relation of the human individual to his group, one can account for this phenomenon, the purposiveness of the larger animal independent of the individuals composing it, only by assuming that individual men have a dual nature, both a group identity and a personal one independent of it but not necessarily in conflict with it.

More must be made of this observation, but in order to do so precisely, it is necessary to restate the earlier relation established between interchapters and plot, using now not the language of determinism and free will but language taken from Steinbeck's quotation above. The content of the interchapters and the content of the plot of *The Grapes of Wrath* relate to each other as the larger animal (the migrant group) to the individuals composing it. The plot portrays members of the school in their rich individuality, whereas the interchapters show the formation of the larger animal that they compose, a formation that takes place both on a de facto level (by virtue of circumstance, a physical group is formed) and on an instinctive one, which endows the animal with life. By virtue of the instinct for self-preservation, in the camps twenty families become one large family, sharing a single instinct. The animal can come to life on this instinctual level because the animal's anlage is in the separate family, the basic unit through which man fulfills his needs, and the instinctual sense of unity is strengthened by a common set of threatening circumstances issuing in shared emotions: first fear, then anger. In this condition, the "school intelligence" directing its drives is instinctual alone, and hence the human group is more like the school of fish to which Steinbeck refers. Guided solely by instinct, the human group-animal achieves a measure of protection from a hostile social environment, but with instinct alone, it can no more transcend the social determinism of the body politic than the turtle (which in the novel symbolizes it in this condition) can transcend the machinations of the drivers eager to squash it. Chance alone can save the group or the turtle as both walk, like Tom, one step ahead of the other, living from day to day.

But the group changes, and in this respect the plot goes one step further than the interchapters, which halt with the fermenting of the grapes of wrath. For the plot shows the emergence of a rational group consciousness, first in Casy, then in Tom, whose final talk with his mother, representing the principle of family, discloses that his own consciousness has transcended such limitations. In fact it is mainly in Tom that the group develops a head for its body; for he survives the murdered Casy, and he was from the beginning more clearly a member of the de facto group than Casy, who owned no land. And by stressing how the animal that is the group achieves rational consciousness and (hence) freedom, Steinbeck harmonizes freedom and determinism in his most important way. The group determined by instinct and circumstance in the interchapters achieves both rational self-awareness and freedom in the person of a member who substitutes the consciousness of a group for a private consciousness and thus gives the group access to the faculty of human will. Tom thus enables it to move from instinct to reason and to that freedom which reasoned acts of the will provide. By having the group consciousness mature in the plot section of his novel, Steinbeck thus unites it to the interchapters structurally and harmonizes his novel philosophically.

And he provides a triumph for the group within the context of determinism, for their attainment of rational group consciousness is itself a determined event because such potential is inherent in the species. Their achieved freedom of will as a group thus is the final term of a socially determined sequence of events that leads to the group's creation, and the group's exercise of it to attain its ends fulfills the historical determinism of the novel. Yet this is not the only hope in these pages, for the prospective triumph of the group provides hope for the triumph of the individual as a whole person.

The Grapes of Wrath is the story of the exploitation of a dispossessed group, and it is difficult not to feel that it will always engender sympathies for the dispossessed of the earth wherever and whenever they might appear. But the novel's indictment of society for what it does to individuals should have an equally enduring appeal; for here its message goes beyond the conditions of oppressed groups and addresses individuals in all strata of complex societies. The condition of individual Oklahomans in fact is an extreme representation of the condition of social man, and in the capacity of individual Oklahomans to change lies the hope for social man.

The migrants' achievement of rational freedom speaks for more than freedom for the group. It tells readers of a vital difference in kinds of freedom. Steinbeck has written, "I believe that man is a double thing—a group animal and at the same time an individual. And it occurs to me that he cannot successfully be the second until he has fulfilled the first." Only the fulfilled group self can create a successful personal self; only freedom exercised by a personal self in harmony with a group self can be significant.

This aspect of the novel's vision depends upon Steinbeck's fuller conception of an individual's two selves. One is his social self, definable by the role he plays in society and by the attitudes he has imbibed from its major institutions. The other is what is best called his species self. It contains all the biological mechanisms—his need for sexual expression, for example—that link him to other creatures in nature. And by virtue of the fact that he is thus linked to the natural world, he can feel a sense of unity with it in its inanimate as well as its animate forms. But the biological element in this self also connects him to the world of man, for it gives him an instinctive sense of identification with other members of his species, just as the members of other species have an instinctive sense of oneness with their own kind.

The species self thus has connections to nonhuman and human nature, and Steinbeck refers to the latter connection when he speaks of man as a "group animal." He views a healthy personal identity as one in which the species self in both its aspects can express itself through the social self of the individual. But society thwarts, or seeks to thwart, the expression of that self. It seeks not only to cut man off from his awareness of his connections to nonhuman nature, it seeks also to sever him from the group sense of oneness with the human species that the individual's species self possesses. Ironically, therefore, purely social man loses a sense of that unity with others which society presumably exists to promote.

The novel's social criticism rests on this view, and its emphasis on grotesques, purely social beings cut off from their connections to nature, both human and nonhuman, portrays an all-too-familiar image of modern man. In too many instances, by imposing mechanical rhythms on human nature, society creates half-men. Its repeated attempts to distort the individual's identity is emphasized by numerous dichotomies between social demands and instinct. Tom tries to comprehend the meaning of his imprisonment for killing in self-defense. Casy tries to understand the meaning of his preaching sexual abstinence when he cannot remain chaste himself. And the point is made by the basic events that set the story moving. A mechanical monster, indifferent to the maternal instincts of the Ma Joads who exercise their species selves in the interest of family solidarity, expels families from their land. The social mechanism thus tries to thwart the demands of the group aspect of the self to remain together. And the same mechanism is responsible for sowing what has become a dust bowl with cotton, rendering it permanently useless for agriculture, thus showing its indifference—nay, hostility—to the connections with nature that the species self feels.

This suppression of the species self is not rigorously foreordained for every individual, and hence the novel's determinism does not rest on the universality of its occurrence. Ma's personality remains undistorted from the novel's beginning to its end. Her intense commitment to the family proceeds from a very live species self; and though she must enlarge her vision to include more than her family, her insistence that Casy join the family on its westward exodus and numerous demonstrations of her concern for others outside her immediate family bear witness that her vision is not all that limited to begin with. But such suppression is nonetheless widespread, and indeed a sufficient number of people must be transformed into grotesques if social structures are to perpetuate themselves. They thereby make many men grotesques and subject all men to economic determinism. Thus the attention to grotesques is part of the pattern of economic determinism in the novel; such determinism can only prevail under conditions guaranteeing with statistical certainty that society can distort man's nature.

The novel singles out two social institutions that assure the creation of grotesques: religion and the law. Lizbeth Sandry is the major representative of a grotesque created by religion. Her intolerance of dancing represents her intolerance of sex, and such intolerance displays religion's warping influence on human instinct. She arouses Ma's ire by warning Rosasharn, "If you got sin on you—you better watch out for that there baby." Her religious views, importing a supernatural mandate into the realm of nature, impose on natural behavior value judgments (like "sin") designed to thwart the normal expression of the species self. This divorce between her social and species selves, indicated by her views, makes Lizbeth Sandry much like one of Sherwood Anderson's grotesques, as all social selves alienated from the species self must be.

Uncle John and Connie's wife, Rosasharn, carry into the family Lizbeth Sandry's fanaticism. Uncle John's felt sense of guilt over his wife's death impels him to blame all the family misfortunes on what he takes to be his sin: his failure to summon a doctor when she complained of physical ailments. His exaggerated sense of sin fails to take into account his own human nature (his natural fallibility) and circumstance; for his reluctance to call a doctor doubtlessly depended on strained finances. His compulsive references to that sin make him as much a grotesque as Lizbeth Sandry, his grotesquerie compounded by his need for wild drinking bouts to escape the sin.

Not only does he become a grotesque, but his obsession with sin blinds Uncle John to the true cause of the family's misfortunes and so shows that religion can indeed be an opiate of the people useful for sustaining an unjust social structure. In this sense Rosasharn is like him, for she has been affected by Lizbeth Sandry's sense of sin. Of course, Rosasharn's sense of sin does not transform her into the grotesque that Uncle John has become. It illustrates that selfishness noted by other critics, for throughout most of the novel she thinks only of herself and her unborn baby, to the total exclusion of the problems of other people. But her view of Tom's killing a deputy, which is one illustration of her selfishness (she shows concern only for her baby, not for her brother), also points to the larger consequences of Uncle John's obsession with sin. She tells Tom, "That lady tol' me. She says what sin's gonna do. . . . An' now you kill a fella. What chance that baby got to get bore right?" Like Uncle John's explanation for family misfortunes, her view of the real-enough threat to her unborn child deflects the source of that threat into a theological realm inaccessible to man, the realm of the devil who tempts man's fallen nature to sin, rather than assigning it to the realm of the accessible and the real, the social forces responsible for the deaths of Casy, the deputy, and her own child.

If religion enforces a split between man's two selves, suppressing one and thus deforming the other, so do most social institutions. Hence the law motif is central to the novel, law being the second (and more important) institution that Steinbeck indicts in his defense of the self; for it is law that holds society's other institutions together and, supported by police power, gives them their governing authority.

References to the law appear in a variety of contexts, but their meaning is best embodied in the opposition between law and fundamental human needs, those " 'got to's' " to which Casy refers that compel men to say, "They's lots a things 'gainst the law that we can't he'p doin.' " Burying Granpa, for example, in defiance of local edict. But there are more important illustrations of how the law thwarts the expression of man's nature, even when it does not manage to distort it. Tom finds no meaning, at the novel's outset, in a system that imprisons him for killing in self-defense, and he discovers the true meaning of the system only after he kills the deputy who murders Casy—a nice bit of symmetry that illustrates his growth in awareness as he perceives, like Casy, that his second killing is also an instinctual response, one of self-defense against the true assaulter, the system, which so thwarts man's instinctual life that it leaves him no choice other than to strike back. This line of meaning is echoed by others: by Ma, who says of Purty Boy Floyd, "He wan't a bad boy. Jus' got drove in a corner"; by the nameless owner men who tell the tenants early in the novel, "You'll be stealing if you try to stay, you'll be murderous if you kill to stay." And it is implicit in Tom's own position at the beginning of the plot: to leave the state violates the conditions of his parole, yet to stay means to break up the family and to face unemployment and possible starvation.

Under such circumstances, it is not surprising to discover that the true prison in *The Grapes of Wrath* is the world outside the prison walls, the real point of Tom's story of a man who deliberately violated parole to return to jail so that he could enjoy the "conveniences" (among them good food) so conspicuously absent in his home. "Here's me, been a-goin' into the wilderness like Jesus to try to find out somepin," Casy says. "Almost got her sometimes, too. But it's in the jail house I really got her." He discovers his proper relationship to men there because it is the place of the free: of men who exercised the natural rights of nature's self only to be imprisoned by the society that resents their exercise. And in fact he can see how the law violates self because he has already seen how religion does. Without the revelations of the wilderness, he would not have had the revelation of the jailhouse; the first is indispensable to the second. Together, they make him the touchstone for understanding the novel's philosophy of self and for measuring the selves of the novel's other characters.

Just as the species self is the ultimate source of freedom for a group, it is the same for an individual. If man can recognize that he is a part of nature by virtue of that self's existence—if he can affirm for this aspect of a naturalistic vision—he can liberate himself from the condition of being a grotesque and, in recognizing his oneness with others, escape the tentacles of economic determinism as well. This is the novel's philosophy of self, and Casy's life is its lived example, both in his thought and in his practice.

Casy has arrived at the vision that man is a part of nature in the novel's opening pages, the discrepancy between his religious preachment and his sexual practice prompting his withdrawal from society to go to the hills in order to comprehend his true relation to the world and leading to his Emersonian sense of connection with nonhuman nature: " 'There was the hills, an' there was me, an' we wasn't separate no more.' " Casy has thus found his deepest nature, that self which is connected even to nonhuman nature, and so he has taken the first vital step toward his liberation. In his way of recovering this self, Casy should be measured less by Emerson than by Thoreau, who went to the woods "to drive life into a corner" and discovered that "not till we are lost . . . , not till we have lost the world, do we begin to find ourselves, and realize where we are and the infinite extent of our relations." For Thoreau, as for Casy and Steinbeck, a true knowledge of the relationship between one's self and the external world can only be derived from an empirical study of the structure of physical reality. Such empiricism imparts the knowledge that man does relate to the whole and inspires, in Steinbeck's words written elsewhere, "the feeling we call religious," the sense of unity between self and outside world that makes "a Jesus, a St. Augustine, a St. Francis, a Roger Bacon, a Charles Darwin, and an Einstein." Writing of his own interest "in relationships of animal to animal," Steinbeck later gave a clue to the general source of the religious vision at which Casy has arrived at the beginning of *The Grapes of Wrath:*

> If one observes in this relational sense, it seems apparent that species are only commas in a sentence, that each species is at once the point and the base of a pyramid, that all life is relational to the point where an Einsteinian relativity seems to emerge. And then not only the meaning but the feeling about species grows misty. One merges into another, groups melt into ecological groups until the time when what we know as life

meets and enters what we think of as non-life: barnacle and rock, rock and earth, earth and tree, tree and rain and air. And the units nestle into the whole and are inseparable from it.

(*Sea of Cortez*)

Any reader of "Song of Myself" would know instantly what Casy and Steinbeck mean. This sense of relationship inspires reverence not for an unknowable God outside of nature but for knowable nature in all its forms; for if one feels united to "the hills," one is clearly in a position to take the next step and feel reverence for nature in its animate forms, and especially in the form known as the human species to which all men belong. And Casy has clearly taken this step as well, as his subsequent remarks on the holiness of man testify. "I got thinkin' how we was holy when we was one thing, an' mankin' was holy when it was one thing." Such human holiness and the consequent sense of human solidarity it engenders come from each man feeling he is "kind of harnessed to the whole shebang," to all of nature. In finding his deepest self, then, Casy has run against the grain of his old social self to embrace a naturalistic religious view which, from Steinbeck's angle of vision, more surely inspires that sense of brotherly love preached by Christianity than Christianity does. A passage from *The Log from the Sea of Cortez* aptly represents the religious view of the novel:

Why do we so dread to think of our species as a species? Can it be that we are afraid of what we may find? That human self-love would suffer too much and that the image of God might prove to be a mask? This could be only partly true, for if we could cease to wear the image of a kindly, bearded, interstellar dictator, we might find ourselves true images of his kingdom, our eyes the nebulae, and universes in our cells.

By descending into his species self, Casy abandons the arrogance of social man who thinks of himself only in terms of his distinctiveness in nature. Specifically, he abandons his social self as preacher and the limitations which it imposes on creating significant relationships with the world outside. As a preacher he necessarily divorced himself from his species self, with its instinctual need for sexual expression, because of Christianity's sexual ethic. Or, rather, since in fact he did act on these instincts, it is more accurate to say that the Christian sexual ethic cut him off from the knowledge that his species self is his better self. Not only does it promote a sense of connection with nature which a Christian sense of man's uniqueness denies—more important, it promotes a sense of connections with all of mankind suppressed by Christianity's parochialism, its division of the world between those who possess the truth and those who live in outer darkness.

Casy's reverence for nature (which also inspires a reverence for human life) allows him to escape character deformations visible in other figures in the novel. Such reverence is markedly absent in men who use their cars to try to run a turtle down, just as it is absent in Al, who swerves his car to squash a snake. When Al becomes "the soul of the car," of course, he is helping his family in their and his time of need, and to that extent the promptings of his species self are very much with him. But its larger sympathies are blunted because the social means by which he is forced to help his family, the automobile on which he must rely, tarnishes him with the taint of "mechanical man," a phrase Steinbeck uses to describe the social man divorced from his species self, and thus accounts for his squashing the snake. In the car he loses contact with that aspect of the species self which reveres life in all its forms, and by so much he becomes a warped victim of society.

Casy escapes this kind of warping because he has established a relationship to the whole, to nonhuman nature. But he also escapes the warping of an Uncle John or a Lizbeth Sandry because he is empirical in establishing a relation to the parts, to the members of the human community which must be man's first concern, as he makes clear when he says, "I ain't gonna preach" and "I ain't gonna baptize":

> I'm gonna work in the fiel's, in the green fiel's an' I'm gonna be near to folks. I ain't gonna try to teach 'em nothin'. I'm gonna try to learn. Gonna learn why the folks walks in the grass, gonna hear 'em talk, gonna hear 'em sing. Gonna listen to kids eatin' mush. Gonna hear husban' an' wife a-poundin' the mattress in the night. Gonna eat with 'em an' learn. . . . All that's holy, all that's what I didn' understan'. All them things is the good things.

Like Thoreau, Casy has reason to believe that most men "have *somewhat hastily* concluded that it is the chief end of man here to 'glorify God and enjoy him forever.' " But his empiricism, not oddly at all, makes him accept in others the very religious view he has already rejected, for such might prove to be the true expression of another's nature. Here he is best measured by Emerson, the Emerson who proclaimed, "Obey thyself," when he tells Uncle John, "I know this—a man got to do what he got to do," or when he says of Uncle John's obsession: "For anybody else it was a mistake, but if you think it was a sin—then it's a sin."

And he follows Emerson in another way. Casy's interest in the parts shows that, like Emerson, he cannot rest satisfied with a religious "high," the feeling of oneness with "the all" that he has already experienced at the novel's opening and that Emerson experienced as "a transparent eyeball." Like Emerson, he must translate the insight derived from that experience into ethical terms on the level of practical action. Having concluded that the devil whom most men should fear is society ("they's somepin worse'n the devil got hold a the country"), he not surprisingly discovers the level of practical action by which he can relate to them in a prison, whose inmates are there mainly " 'cause they stole stuff; an' mostly it was stuff they needed an' couldn' get no other way. . . . It's need that makes all the trouble." Since society cannot provide man's basic needs, Casy will help to secure them and, in the process, he brings his species self into relation with men by adopting a social one that permits its expression. He becomes a strike organizer.

Casy's new personal identity is thus an expression of a larger self which, as Emerson knew, can be realized in a diverse number of concrete social forms, though such self-realization earns the world's displeasure. Members of the family who remain in the group thus move toward that larger self when they abandon older views of theological sin as a causal factor in human affairs and approximate Casy's newer view in their words and actions. Uncle John displays this movement, his escape from the ranks of the grotesque, when he floats Rosasharn's stillborn baby to the town, admonishing it to "go down in the street an' rot an' tell 'em that way," just as Rosasharn does when she breastfeeds the old man in the novel's closing paragraph. Her gesture acknowledges the truth of Uncle John's words, that the sin that killed her baby was social and not theological in origin. The same gesture shows her overcoming a solipsism engendered by her pregnancy by enlarging the sympathies of her species self to embrace more than the child that society denied her. That gesture, finally, is the perfect one to signal the awakening of nature's self, the self growing from that human biological nature which mothers and fathers the species.

The novel thus suggests the desirability of a society based not on absolutes imported supernaturally into nature by systems derived from a priori thinking, but one whose institutions accommodate themselves to subjective absolutes. In this way Steinbeck's novel expands the naturalistic vision of *Manhattan Transfer*. It develops the theme only subordinate in the earlier novel: man and nature are one, not two. But *The Grapes of*

Wrath is also a logical and satisfying conclusion to naturalism prior to Dos Passos. If man's connections to nonhuman nature seemed a source of savagery for Crane, nonetheless, at the last, nature in "The Open Boat" was just nature—a vast system for man to interpret for his own benefit, could he but escape the complicated social fabric to see that the primary purpose of societies is to aid him in creating such interpretations. Even in *McTeague,* brute nature is not entirely without its redeeming values: it alone provides McTeague with the sixth sense to flee the city that so twists the lives of the people in Norris's pages. Because the novel is so completely deterministic, however, nature is not used as an avenue of escape. In its form as sexual drive, it instead contributes to McTeague's destruction. But for Steinbeck, nature did become a viable avenue of escape when he developed a religious vision based on the feeling resulting from empirically ascertainable knowledge, the knowledge that man is related to the vast system called Nature. This vision is implicit in Dreiser's view of a creative spirit, but unlike Dreiser, Steinbeck postulates no unknowable purpose in this spirit possibly running at cross-purposes to man's own. He escapes the tentacles of determinism that hold Dreiser's men and women in thrall because he does not unravel the Hobbesian dilemma; because he does not reduce consciousness to temperament or instinct; because he instead makes consciousness in the service of man's instinct the center of man's freedom. Like Emerson, and Dreiser at the last, he assumes that if nature's spirit has purpose, man as part of it can give it expression and direction by realizing his own purpose. To attain knowledge of this ability is to begin to meet the demands of spring.

ANTHONY BURGESS

Living for Writing

Hemingway was, and is still, Steinbeck's trouble. When Steinbeck was struggling to become a novelist, somebody recommended that he read Hemingway's short stories. He read "The Killers" and was stunned. Here, he said, was the finest writer alive; he did not dare to read any more of him. Only when his own reputation was secured with *The Grapes of Wrath* did he feel free to read the rest of Hemingway. He even agreed, later, to meet him. But Hemingway behaved badly, as usual, and, denying that the blackthorn stick Steinbeck had given to John O'Hara was, even though it had been long in the Steinbeck family, really blackthorn, broke it over his own head. O'Hara, who was perhaps on the same level of attainment as Steinbeck, or somewhat lower, had the same truculent and jealous admiration for Hemingway, expressed in denigratory snarls. It was worse for O'Hara, who did not get the Nobel Prize and, unlike Steinbeck, desperately wanted it. But Steinbeck would sometimes pause in his peeling of onions for the "great chilli" he used to make, take *The Sun Also Rises* from the shelf, and sneer at Hemingway's dialogue. This was not altogether in character. Mr Benson expends 1100 pages on showing us what a nice man Steinbeck was.

Though the Nobel raised him to Hemingway's level in the world's eyes (and to Galsworthy's, Pearl Buck's, and Golding's), Steinbeck remains a worthy rather than an important writer. Neither he nor O'Hara did what Hemingway did—stripped language to the nerve, created a new and very twentieth-century kind of stoicism, entered the stream of European

From *But Do Blondes Prefer Gentlemen? Homage to Qwert Yuiop and Other Writings*. © 1986 by Liana Burgess. McGraw-Hill, 1986.

modernism in order to make it American. Mr Benson seems, in [the] early pages [of his biography, *The True Adventures of John Steinbeck, Writer*], to be writing about a highly innovative novelist, like Galdós, when he says: "Early in his career he was interested in trying to imitate the structure and movement of specific musical compositions, as well as more generally trying to imitate certain musical forms." Whatever his early ambitions, Steinbeck owed his success to a very orthodox kind of fiction with traditional prose rhythms, whose power resided in a subject matter always highly emotional and sometimes topically inflammatory.

Of Mice and Men is, I think, a fine novella (or play with extended stage directions) which succeeds because it dares sentimentality. We remember it best as a film with Burgess Meredith and Lon Chaney Jr ("Tell about the rabbits, George"), just as we remember that saga of the oppressed and wandering Okies, *The Grapes of Wrath*, for the performance of Henry Fonda, and *East of Eden* as a vehicle for the doomed and brilliant James Dean. Steinbeck was always luckier than Hemingway in his film adaptations. He loved the medium and he did good work for it: his *Viva Zapata!* is masterly. He loved it because he had a gift for dialogue but no corresponding talent for a modern kind of *récit:* in film, *récit* is left to the camera. Hemingway's dialogue is less realistic than it looks, but his *récit* is nerve and bone and very original and new.

The Grapes of Wrath was a bestseller because it was a cry of referred pain. The migrants from the Dust Bowl were being wretchedly exploited by the California fruit farmers, who chained them to the company store and kept them only just floating at a level of bestial subsistence. The book looked like radical propaganda of the kind that Hemingway, to the disgust of *New Masses,* always refused to write, but Steinbeck insisted that the endpapers show a reproduction of "The Battle Hymn of the Republic," whence his title came, and maintained stoutly and ever that he was a Jeffersonian Democrat who detested the very idea of communism. When, in later life, he visited Russia, he was not slow to knock the Soviet system. Sending dispatches from Vietnam, he had to struggle between detestation of the war and loyalty to his President. He was a man of simple honour, and it shows in his books.

When the Nobel confirmed that he had done his best work, Steinbeck began to see that he stood for an outmoded ethic. His later days were spent in a kind of dogged futility, soaking in the Arthurian legends— mostly on the spot, near Cadbury, with the great Professor Vinaver to help him—in order to rewrite them and relate them to the modern age. He couldn't do it, but he tried hard. He was always the dedicated writer, and it pained him that the image of the debased and self-glorifying Hemingway had somehow rubbed on to him. He was supposed to be a hard drinker, but he drank little. He had only three wives. He did not like being famous. Compared with Hemingway, whose fists and corridas and safaris get in the way of his prose, he had few adventures, and the title of his biography rings ironically.

Hemingway, secure in his Anglo-Saxon ancestry, could mock his name into Hemingstein. Steinbeck was assumed by the Nazis to be a Jew, especially when he wrote the anti-totalitarian *The Moon Is Down,* a copy of which it was death to possess in occupied Europe. He was in fact a mixture of Ulster Irish and German Lutheran, and the mission of his Düsseldorf forebears had been to convert the Jews to laborious Protestantism. The family settled in Salinas, California, and it is safe to consider Steinbeck a regional novelist whose best work has a Californian locale— the fruit farms with their sweated immigrant labour, the coast at Monterey. California brought him close to the Mexicans, eventually to Zapata. He never felt much inclination to drink of the European stream, like Hemingway. Joyce did not, apparently, excite him. The rural nostalgia of *East of Eden* finds very orthodox expression:

> Under the live oaks, shaded and dusky, the maidenhair flourished and gave a good smell, and under the mossy banks of the water courses whole clumps of five-fingered ferns and goldybacks hung down. Then there were harebells, tiny lanterns, cream white and almost sinful looking, and these were so rare and magical that a child, finding one, felt singled out and special all day long.

I have just published a novella in which, by happy chance, Steinbeck is mentioned. " 'I met Steinbeck,' Enderby said, 'when he was given, unjustly I thought and still think, the Nobel, oh I don't know though when you consider some of these dago scribblers who get it, think it was an unjust bestowal. There was a party for him given by Heinemann in London. I asked him what he was going to do with the prize money and he said: *fuck off.*' " The party goes unmentioned by Mr Benson (who has otherwise recorded every pimple and mouthful). What Steinbeck said to Enderby he really said to me. The rudeness was not typical but Steinbeck was very tired. Before then he had been a very tireless writer. It is a great deal to say of a writer that he lived for writing. Steinbeck did.

LOUIS OWENS

Of Mice and Men:
The Dream of Commitment

The Eden myth looms large in *Of Mice and Men* (1937), the play-novella set along the Salinas River "a few miles south of Soledad." And, as in all of Steinbeck's California fiction, setting plays a central role in determining the major themes of this work. The fact that the setting for *Of Mice and Men* is a California valley dictates, according to the symbolism of Steinbeck's landscapes, that this story will take place in a fallen world and that the quest for the illusive and illusory American Eden will be of central thematic significance. In no other work does Steinbeck demonstrate greater skill in merging the real setting of his native country with the thematic structure of his novel.

Critics have consistently recognized in Lennie's dream of living "off the fatta the lan' " on a little farm the American dream of a new Eden. Joseph Fontenrose states concisely, "The central image is the earthly paradise. . . . It is a vision of Eden." Peter Lisca takes this perception further, noting that "the world of *Of Mice and Men* is a fallen one, inhabited by sons of Cain, forever exiled from Eden, the little farm of which they dream." There are no Edens in Steinbeck's writing, only illusions of Eden, and in the fallen world of the Salinas Valley—which Steinbeck would later place "east of Eden"—the Promised Land is an illusory and painful dream. In this land populated by "sons of Cain," men condemned to wander in solitude, the predominant theme is that of loneliness, or what Donald Pizer has called "fear of apartness." Pizer has,

From *John Steinbeck's Re-Vision of America.* © 1985 by the University of Georgia Press.

in fact, discovered *the* major theme of this novel when he says, "One of the themes of *Of Mice and Men* is that men fear loneliness, that they need someone to be with and to talk to who will offer understanding and companionship."

The setting Steinbeck chose for this story brilliantly underscores the theme of man's isolation and need for commitment. Soledad is a very real, dusty little town on the western edge of the Salinas River midway down the Salinas Valley. Like most of the settings in Steinbeck's fiction, this place exists, it *is*. However, with his acute sensitivity to place names and his knowledge of Spanish, Steinbeck was undoubtedly aware that "Soledad" translates into English as "solitude" or "loneliness." In this country of solitude and loneliness, George and Lennie stand out sharply because they have each other or, as George says, "We got somebody to talk to that gives a damn about us." Cain's question is the question again at the heart of this novel: "Am I my brother's keeper?" And the answer found in the relationship between George and Lennie is an unmistakable confirmation.

Of Mice and Men is most often read as one of Steinbeck's most pessimistic works, smacking of pessimistic determinism. Fontenrose suggests that the novel is about "the vanity of human wishes" and asserts that, more pessimistically than Burns, "Steinbeck reads, '*All* schemes o' mice and men gan *ever* agley' " [my italics]. Howard Levant, in a very critical reading of the novel, concurs, declaring that "the central theme is stated and restated—the good life is impossible because humanity is flawed." In spite of the general critical reaction, and without disputing the contention that Steinbeck allows no serious hope that George and Lennie will ever acheive their dream farm, it is nonetheless possible to read *Of Mice and Men* in a more optimistic light than has been customary. In previous works we have seen a pattern established in which the Steinbeck hero achieves greatness in the midst of, even because of, apparent defeat. In *Of Mice and Men,* Steinbeck accepts, very nonteleologically, the fact that man is flawed and the Eden myth mere illusion. However, critics have consistently under-valued Steinbeck's emphasis on the theme of commitment, which runs through the novel and which is the chief ingredient in the creation of the Steinbeck hero.

The dream of George and Lennie represents a desire to defy the curse of Cain and fallen man—to break the pattern of wandering and loneliness imposed on the outcasts and to return to the perfect garden. George and Lennie achieve all of this dream that is possible in the real world: they are their brother's keepers. Unlike the solitary Cain and the solitary men who inhabit the novel, they have someone who cares. The dream of the farm merely symbolizes their deep mutual commitment, a commitment that is immediately sensed by the other characters in the novel. The ranch owner is suspicious of the relationship, protesting, "I never seen one guy take so much trouble for another guy." Slim, the godlike jerkline skinner, admires the relationship and says, "Ain't many guys travel around together. . . . I don't know why. Maybe everybody in the whole damn world is scared of each other." Candy, the one-handed swamper, and Crooks, the deformed black stablehand, also sense the unique commitment between the two laborers, and in their moment of unity Candy and Crooks turn as one to defend Lennie from the threat posed by Curley's wife. The influence of George and Lennie's mutual commitment, and of their dream, has for an instant made these crippled sons of Cain their brother's keepers and broken the grip of loneliness and solitude in which they exist. Lennie's yearning for the rabbits and for all soft, living things symbolizes the yearning all men have for warm, living contact. It is this yearning, described by Steinbeck as "the inarticulate and powerful yearning of all men," which makes George need Lennie just as much as Lennie needs George and which sends Curley's wife wandering despairingly about the ranch in search of companionship. Whereas Fontenrose has suggested that "the individualistic desire for carefree enjoyment of pleasures is the serpent in the garden" in this book, the real serpent is loneliness and the barriers between men and between men and women that create and reinforce this loneliness.

Lennie has been seen as representing "the frail nature of primeval innocence" and as the id to George's ego or the body to George's brain. In the novel, Lennie is repeatedly associated with animals or described as childlike. He appears in the opening scene dragging his feet "the way a bear drags his paws," and in the final scene he enters the clearing in the brush "as silently as a creeping bear." Slim says of Lennie, "He's jes' like a kid, ain't he," and George repeats, "Sure, he's jes' like a kid." The unavoidable truth is, however, that Lennie, be he innocent "natural," uncontrollable id, or simply a huge child, is above all dangerous. Unlike Benjy in *The Sound and the Fury* (whom Steinbeck may have had in mind when describing the incident in Weed in which Lennie clings bewildered to the girl's dress), Lennie is monstrously powerful and has a propensity for killing things. Even if Lennie had not killed Curley's wife, he would sooner or later have done something fatal to bring violence upon himself, as the lynch mob that hunted him in Weed suggests.

Steinbeck's original title for *Of Mice and Men* was "Something That Happened," a title suggesting that Steinbeck was taking a purly nonteleological or nonblaming point of view in this novel. If we look at the novel in this way, it becomes clear that Lennie dies because he has been created incapable of dealing with society and is, in fact, a menace to society. Like Pepé in "Flight," Tularecito in *The Pastures of Heaven,* and Frankie in *Cannery Row,* Lennie is a "natural" who loses when he is forced to confront society. This is simply the way it is—something that happened—and when George kills Lennie he is not only saving him from the savagery of the pursuers, he is, as John Ditsky says, acknowledging that "Lennie's situation is quite hopeless." Ditsky further suggests that Lennie's death represents "a matter of cold hard necessity imposing itself upon the frail hopes of man." Along these same lines, Joan Steele declares that "Lennie has to be destroyed because he is a 'loner' whose weakness precludes his cooperating with George and hence working constructively toward their mutual goal." Lennie, however, is not a "loner"; it is, in fact, the opposite, overwhelming and uncontrollable urge for contact that brings about Lennie's destruction and the destruction of living creatures he comes into contact with. Nonetheless, Steele makes an important point when she suggests that because of Lennie the dream of the Edenic farm was never a possibility. Lennie's flaw represents the inherent imperfection in humanity that renders Eden forever an impossibility. Lennie would have brought his imperfection with him to the little farm, and he would have killed the rabbits.

When Lennie dies, the teleological dream of the Edenic farm dies with him, for while Lennie's weakness doomed the dream it was only his innocence that kept it alive. The death of the dream, however, does not force *Of Mice and Men* to end on the strong note of pessimism critics have consistently claimed. For while the dream of the farm perishes, the theme of commitment achieves its strongest statement in the book's conclusion. Unlike Candy, who abandons responsibility for his old dog and allows Carlson to shoot him, George remains his brother's keeper without faltering even to the point of killing Lennie while Lennie sees visions of Eden. In accepting complete responsibility for Lennie, George demonstrates the degree of commitment necessary to the Steinbeck hero, and in fact enters the ranks of those heroes. It is ironic that, in this fallen world, George must reenact the crime of Cain to demonstrate the depth of his commitment. It is a frank acceptance of the way things are.

Slim recognizes the meaning of George's act. When the pursuers discover George just after he has shot Lennie, Steinbeck writes: "Slim came directly to George and sat down beside him, sat very close to him." Steinbeck's forceful prose here, with the key word "directly," and the emphatic repetition in the last phrase place heavy emphasis on Slim's gesture. Steinbeck is stressing the significance of the new relationship between George and Slim. As the novel ends, George is going off with Slim to have a drink, an action Fontenrose mistakenly interprets as evidence "that George had turned to his counterdream of independence: freedom from Lennie." French suggests that "Slim's final attempt to console George ends the novel on the same compassionate note as that of *The Red Pony,* but Slim can only alleviate, not cure, the situation." Steinbeck, however, seems to be deliberately placing much greater emphasis on the developing friendship between the two men than such interpretations would allow for. Lisca has pointed out the circular structure of the novel—the neat balancing of the opening and closing scenes. Bearing this circularity in mind, it should be noted that this novel about man's loneliness and "apartness" began with two men—George and Lennie—climbing down to the pool from the highway and that the novel ends with two men—George and Slim—climbing back up from the pool to the highway. Had George been left alone and apart from the rest of humanity at the end of the novel, had he suffered the fate of Cain, this would indeed have been the most pessimistic of Steinbeck's works. That George is not alone has tremendous significance. In the fallen world of the valley, where human commitment is the only realizable dream, the fact that in the end as in the beginning two men walk together causes *Of Mice and Men* to end on a strong note of hope—the crucial dream, the dream of man's commitment to man, has not perished with Lennie. The dream will appear again, in fact, in much greater dimension in Steinbeck's next novel, *The Grapes of Wrath.*

Abra: The Indestructible Woman
in East of Eden

By the end of the 1940s Steinbeck was ready to attempt another big book, a book with the rather ambitious purpose of not only telling the story of his family but of "the whole nasty bloody lovely history of the world." In that story women play a significant role. Cathy/Kate, who is both Terrible Mother and Duplicitous Eve in one, dominates most of the novel. Hers is the character who fascinates readers; she is the character about whom the plot of fraternal rivalry revolves. The major female figure in this generational saga is a monster, perhaps the most vituperative villainess in American fiction. She occupies both of the categories Steinbeck reserves for women; she is both a mother and a whore. But, contrary to his usual sentimentalization of these roles, Steinbeck shows Cathy as a malevolent mother, one who tries to abort and then abandons her children. She is also a far cry from his usual whore with a heart of gold.

The myth that underlies *East of Eden* is the Cain and Abel story, the archetype for sibling rivalry and fratricide. Steinbeck identifies himself and all of us, since we are all the children of Cain, with Cal, the Cain figure who indirectly causes the death of his brother. Cal must learn about his nature and about his choices in life. The operative theme is the concept of "timshel," God's injunction to Cain which either commands him to triumph over evil or gives him the choice to do so. Caleb chooses redemption, but he does not do it alone. He is strongly supported by Abra, one of Stein-

From *The Indestructible Woman in Faulkner, Hemingway and Steinbeck*. © 1986 by Mimi Reisel Gladstein. UMI Research Press, 1986.

beck's most positively depicted women. *East of Eden* is a novel with an optimistic conclusion and Abra is instrumental in that outcome.

Steinbeck's purpose in creating the character of Abra is in no way ambiguous. He tells us in *Journal of a Novel: The* East of Eden *Letters* that he intends for her to represent "the strong female principle of good." She is to be "a fighter and an effective human being." Steinbeck succeeds admirably. Abra is an appealing character, good and yet realistically human. Steinbeck tells us in his narrator's commentary that there is only one story in the world and that that is the "never-ending contest in ourselves of good and evil." Abra, who is very much aware of the bad in herself, consciously chooses the good. Not only does she choose a positive role for herself, but she encourages Cal in that direction also. When he would hide from the terrible reality of his actions and his father's illness by returning to the womblike security of the "sweetly protected and warm and safe" envelopment of the willow tree, she forces him home instead.

Abra's good judgment is inherent. Even as a little girl she is described as having "wisdom and sweetness in her expression." When she and Aron are both children, she mothers him and treats him with "condescending wisdom." In their play she wants to pretend to be his wife, but Aron wants her to be the mother he never had, a role she slips into easily. She coos at Aron, "Come, my baby, put your head in Mother's lap." Lee, the novel's resident sage, understands her inherent maturity when he calls the teen-aged Abra "a good woman—a real woman." Cal counters that she is a girl, but Lee corrects him. "No. . . . A few are women from the moment they're born. Abra has the loveliness of woman, and the courage—and the strength—and the wisdom."

In his description of Abra, Steinbeck makes observations about women's ability to focus on the larger picture, the eternal rather than temporal view, which are similar to some of Faulkner's. When Aron plunges into a religious fervor, we are told Abra's reaction by the narrator: "Her feminine mind knew that such things were necessary but unimportant." When Aron chooses celibacy, "Abra in her wisdom agreed with him, feeling and hoping that this phase would pass." Abra is able to take the long view, to see beyond the exigencies of the moment at the tender age of fourteen, a rare feat.

If the reader is to accept Steinbeck's contemporary rendering of the Cain and Abel myth as representative of the "whole nasty bloody lovely history of the world," then Abra as a second Eve is also a prototype for the feminine. The adjective that Steinbeck uses most often to characterize her is strong. Besides the descriptions of her already cited, the narrator also pictures her as "straight, strong, fine-breasted," and in another instance her "strength and goodness" and "warmth" are specified. She is womanly, but it is a womanliness of "bold muscular strength."

Abra does not shrink from her womanly role. She rejects Aron's desire to idealize her, to turn her into a "Goddess-Virgin." She does not want to be an ethereal being, the angel woman of Aron's fantasies. She wants to be a sexual being, a biological mother in a relationship with a man who sees her as a flesh and blood human being rather than one who has created his own version of her. The prognosis for her future is a good one. In the final scene of the novel Lee is trying to communicate to Adam the importance of his forgiving Cal and giving him his blessing. He brings Cal and Abra into the room with him and points out to Adam that Cal's and Abra's children "will be the only remnant left of you." With great effort Adam provides that blessing by uttering the reinforcing word "timshel," the word that communicates to Cal that he can choose to triumph over the sin he has committed and live a good and full life with Abra.

Chronology

1902	John Ernst Steinbeck born February 27 in Salinas, California.
1919	Graduates from Salinas High School.
1920–25	Attends Stanford and works as laborer intermittently. Publishes first short stories in *The Stanford Spectator*.
1925	Drops out of Stanford and goes to New York. Works as construction laborer and reports for the *American*.
1926	Returns to California, writes stories and novels.
1929	*Cup of Gold* published.
1930	Marries Carol Henning and settles in Pacific Grove. Meets Edward F. Ricketts, a marine biologist.
1932	*The Pastures of Heaven*. Moves to Los Angeles.
1933	*To a God Unknown*. Returns to Monterey. *The Red Pony* appears in two parts in *North American Review*.
1934	"The Murder" wins the O. Henry Prize.
1935	*Tortilla Flat* published.
1936	*In Dubious Battle*. Steinbeck travels to Mexico.
1937	*Of Mice and Men*. *The Red Pony* in three parts. Travels to Europe and later from Oklahoma to California with migrants.
1938	*The Long Valley*.
1939	*The Grapes of Wrath*, which wins the Pulitzer Prize.
1940	Sets out with Ricketts to collect marine invertebrates in the Gulf of California.

1941　*Sea of Cortez* published, with Edward F. Ricketts.

1942　*The Moon Is Down.* Steinbeck divorces Carol Henning. *Bombs Away* written for the U.S. Air Force.

1943　Marries Gwendolyn Conger and moves to New York. In Europe covering the war as correspondent for *The New York Herald Tribune.*

1944　Writes script for Alfred Hitchcock's *Lifeboat.* Son Thomas born.

1945　*Cannery Row. The Red Pony* with fourth part, "The Leader of the People." "The Pearl of the World" appears in *Women's Home Companion.*

1946　Son John born.

1947　Travels in Russia with photographer Robert Capa. *The Wayward Bus. The Pearl.*

1948　*A Russian Journal.* Divorces Gwendolyn Conger. Edward Ricketts is killed in a car-train crash.

1950　*Burning Bright.* Writes script for *Viva Zapata!* Marries Elaine Scott.

1951　*The Log from the Sea of Cortez,* with a preface about Edward Ricketts.

1952　*East of Eden.*

1954　*Sweet Thursday.*

1957　*The Short Reign of Pippin IV.*

1958　*Once There Was a War,* a collection of war dispatches.

1960　Steinbeck takes a three month tour of America with his dog, Charley.

1961　*The Winter of Our Discontent.*

1962　*Travels with Charley in Search of America.* Wins the Nobel Prize for literature.

1964　Awarded United States Medal of Freedom.

1965　Reports from Vietnam for *Newsday.*

1966   *America and Americans.*

1968   Dies December 20, buried in Salinas.

1969   *Journals of a Novel: The* East of Eden *Letters.*

1976   *The Acts of King Arthur and His Noble Knights.*

Contributors

HAROLD BLOOM, Sterling Professor of the Humanities at Yale University, is the author of *The Anxiety of Influence, Poetry and Repression,* and many other volumes of literary criticism. His forthcoming study, *Freud: Transference and Authority,* attempts a full-scale reading of all of Freud's major writings. A MacArthur Prize Fellow, he is general editor of five series of literary criticism published by Chelsea House. During 1987–88, he was appointed Charles Eliot Norton Professor of Poetry at Harvard University.

DONALD WEEKS has written on Yeats, Shelley, and Steinbeck.

RICHARD ASTRO is Dean of the College of Arts and Sciences at Northeastern University. He is the author of *John Steinbeck and Edward F. Ricketts: The Shaping of a Novelist.*

HOWARD LEVANT is the author of *The Novels of John Steinbeck.*

WARREN FRENCH is Professor of English at Indiana University-Purdue University. His books include *The Social Novel at the End of an Era,* and studies of Frank Norris and J. D. Salinger.

ARTHUR F. KINNEY is Professor of English at Clark University. He has written widely on Steinbeck, Faulkner, and Auden, and is the author of several books on Shakespeare and Elizabethan drama.

MARILYN L. MITCHELL teaches English at Wayne State University.

JACKSON J. BENSON is Professor of English and Comparative Literature at San Diego State University. His books include *The True Adventures of John Steinbeck, Writer: A Biography.*

JOHN J. CONDER is Associate Professor of English at Vanderbilt University. He is the author of *Naturalism in American Fiction: The Classic Phase.*

ANTHONY BURGESS is writer-in-residence at the Grimaldi Palace in Monaco, and is the author of *A Clockwork Orange, Earthly Powers,* and the Enderby novels. His criticism includes a study of D. H. Lawrence and two books on Joyce.

LOUIS OWENS teaches English at California State University, Northridge. He is the author of *John Steinbeck's Re-Vision of America.*

MIMI REISEL GLADSTEIN is Associate Professor of English at the University of Texas, El Paso, and the author of *The Indestructible Woman in Faulkner, Hemingway, and Steinbeck.*

Bibliography

Aaron, Daniel. *Writers on the Left.* New York: Harcourt, Brace & World, 1961.
———. "The Radical Humanism of John Steinbeck." *Saturday Review,* 28 September 1968.
Alexander, Stanley. "The Conflict of Form in *Tortilla Flat.*" *American Literature* 40 (1968): 58–60.
Astro, Richard. *John Steinbeck and Edward F. Ricketts: The Shaping of a Novelist.* Minneapolis: University of Minnesota Press, 1973.
Baker, Carlos. "*In Dubious Battle* Revalued." *New York Times Book Review,* 5 July 1943.
Benson, Jackson J. " 'To Tom, Who Lived It': John Steinbeck and the Man from Weedpatch." *Journal of Modern Literature* 5 (1976): 151–94.
———. *The True Adventures of John Steinbeck, Writer: A Biography.* New York: Viking, 1983.
Carpenter, F. I. "John Steinbeck: The Philosophical Joads." *College English* 2 (1941): 315–25.
Davis, Robert Murray, ed. *Steinbeck: A Collection of Critical Essays.* Englewood Cliffs, N.J.: Prentice-Hall, 1972.
Ditsky, John. "Words and Deeds in *Viva Zapata!*" *Dalhousie Review* 56 (1976): 125–31.
———. "Ritual Murder in Steinbeck's Dramas." *Steinbeck Quarterly* 11 (Summer–Fall 1978): 72–76.
———. "The Ending of *The Grapes of Wrath:* A Reconsideration." *Southern Humanities Review* 13 (1979): 215–20.
Fontenrose, Joseph. *John Steinbeck: An Introduction and Interpretation.* New York: Barnes & Noble, 1963.
French, Warren. *The Social Novel at the End of an Era.* Carbondale: Southern Illinois University Press, 1966.
———. *John Steinbeck.* Rev. ed. Boston: Twayne, 1975.
———. "John Steinbeck and Modernism." In *Steinbeck's Prophetic Vision of America: Proceedings of the Bicentennial Steinbeck Seminar,* edited by Tetsumaro Hayashi and Kenneth D. Swan. Upland, Ind.: Taylor University for the John Steinbeck Society of America, 1976.
Garcia, Reloy. *Steinbeck and D. H. Lawrence: Fictive Voices and the Ethical Imperative.* Muncie, Ind.: The John Steinbeck Society of America, 1972.
Geismar, Maxwell. "John Steinbeck: Of Wrath of Joy." In *Writers in Crisis:*

The American Novel: 1925–1940, 237–70. Boston: Houghton Mifflin, 1942.

Gray, James. *John Steinbeck*. Minneapolis: University of Minnesota Press, 1971.

Hayashi, Tetsumaro. *Steinbeck's Literary Dimension: A Guide to Comparative Studies*. Metuchen, N.J.: Scarecrow Press, 1973.

———. *Steinbeck Criticism: A Review of Book-Length Studies*. Muncie, Ind.: The John Steinbeck Society of America, 1974.

———, ed. *Steinbeck and the Arthurian Theme*. Muncie, Ind.: The John Steinbeck Society of America, 1975.

———, ed. *Steinbeck's Women: Essays in Criticism*. Muncie, Ind.: The John Steinbeck Society of America, 1979.

———, ed. *Steinbeck's Travel Literature: Essays in Criticism*. Muncie, Ind.: The John Steinbeck Society of America, 1980.

Hyman, Stanley Edgar. "Some Notes on John Steinbeck." *Antioch Review* 2 (1942): 185–200.

Jones, Lawrence William. *John Steinbeck as Fabulist*. Edited by Marston LaFrance. Muncie, Ind.: The John Steinbeck Society of America, 1973.

Justus, James H. "The Transient World of *Tortilla Flat*." *Western Review* 7, no. 1 (1970): 55–60.

Kazin, Alfred. *On Native Grounds: An Interpretation of Modern American Prose Literature*. New York: Anchor Books, 1956.

Kiernan, Thomas. *The Intricate Music: A Biography of John Steinbeck*. Boston: Little, Brown, 1979.

Levant, Howard. "*Tortilla Flat*: The Shape of John Steinbeck's Career." *PMLA* 85 (1970): 1087–95.

———. *The Novels of John Steinbeck: A Critical Study*. Columbia: University of Missouri Press, 1974.

Lieber, Todd M. "Talismanic Patterns in the Novels of John Steinbeck." *American Literature* 44 (1972): 262–75.

Lisca, Peter. *The Wide World of John Steinbeck*. New Brunswick, N.J.: Rutgers University Press, 1958.

———. "The Dynamics of Community in *The Grapes of Wrath*." In *From Irving to Steinbeck: Studies of American Literature in Honor of Harry R. Warfel*, edited by Motley Deakin and Peter Lisca. Gainesville: University of Florida Press, 1972.

———. *John Steinbeck: Nature and Myth*. New York: Crowell, 1978.

———, ed. The Grapes of Wrath: *Text and Criticism*. New York: Viking, 1972.

McCarthy, Paul. *John Steinbeck*. New York: Frederick Ungar, 1980.

Magny, Claude-Edmonde. "Steinbeck, or the Limits of the Impersonal Novel." In *The Age of the American Novel: The Film Aesthetic of Fiction Between the Two Wars*, 161–77. New York: Frederick Ungar, 1972.

Marks, Lester Jay. *Thematic Design in the Novels of John Steinbeck*. The Hague: Mouton, 1969.

Metzger, Charles R. "Steinbeck's Version of the Pastoral." *Modern Fiction Studies* 6 (1960): 115–24.

Modern Fiction Studies 11 (1965). Special John Steinbeck issue.

Moore, Harry Thornton. *The Novels of John Steinbeck: A First Critical Study.* Chicago: Normandie House, 1939.

O'Connor, Richard. *John Steinbeck.* New York: McGraw-Hill, 1970.

Owens, Louis. *John Steinbeck's Re-Vision of America.* Athens: University of Georgia Press, 1985.

Pizer, Donald. "John Steinbeck and American Naturalism." *Steinbeck Quarterly* 9 (Winter 1976): 12–15.

Pollock, Theodore. "On the Ending of *The Grapes of Wrath.*" *Modern Fiction Studies* 4 (1958): 177–78.

St. Pierre, Brian. *John Steinbeck: The California Years.* San Francisco: Chronicle Books, 1983.

Salter, Christopher L. "John Steinbeck's *The Grapes of Wrath* as a Primer for Cultural Geography." In *Humanistic Geography and Literature: Essays on the Experience of Place,* edited by Douglas C. Pocock. London: Croom Helm, 1981.

Simmonds, Roy S. *Steinbeck's Literary Achievements.* Muncie, Ind.: The John Steinbeck Society of America, 1976.

Steele, Joan. "A Century of Idiots: *Barnaby Rudge* and *Of Mice and Men.*" *Steinbeck Quarterly* 5 (Winter 1972): 8–17.

Steinbeck Quarterly, 1967–.

Taylor, Walter Fuller. "*The Grapes of Wrath* Reconsidered." *Mississippi Quarterly: The Journal of Southern Culture* 12 (1959): 136–44.

Tedlock, E. W., Jr., and C. V. Wicker, eds. *Steinbeck and His Critics: A Record of Twenty-Five Years.* Albuquerque: University of New Mexico Press, 1957.

Watkins, Floyd C. "Flat Wine from *The Grapes of Wrath.*" In *The Humanist in His World: Essays in Honor of Fielding Dillard Russell,* edited by Barbara W. Bitter and Frederick K. Sanders. Greenwood, S.C.: Attic, 1976.

Watt, F. W. *John Steinbeck.* New York: Grove Press, 1962.

Wilson, Edmund. "The Boys in the Back Room." In *Classics and Commercials,* 35–45. New York: Farrar & Straus, 1950.

Zollman, Sol. "John Steinbeck's Political Outlook in *The Grapes of Wrath.*" *Literature and Ideology* (Montreal) 13 (1972): 9–20.

Acknowledgments

"Steinbeck Against Steinbeck" by Donald Weeks from *The Pacific Spectator* 1, no. 4 (Autumn 1947), © 1947 by the Pacific Coast Committee for the Humanities of the American Council of Learned Societies. Reprinted by permission.

"Intimations of a Wasteland" by Richard Astro from *John Steinbeck and Edward F. Ricketts: The Shaping of a Novelist* by Richard Astro, © 1973 by the University of Minnesota. Reprinted by permission of the University of Minnesota Press.

"The Fully Matured Art: *The Grapes of Wrath*" by Howard Levant from *The Novels of John Steinbeck: A Critical Study* by Howard Levant, © 1974 by the Curators of the University of Missouri. Reprinted by permission of the University of Missouri Press.

"John Steinbeck: A Usable Concept of Naturalism" by Warren French from *American Literary Naturalism: A Reassessment,* edited by Yoshinobu Hakutani and Lewis Fried, © 1975 by Warren French. Reprinted by permission of the author and Carl Winter Universitäts Verlag.

"*Tortilla Flat* Re-Visited" by Arthur F. Kinney from *Steinbeck and the Arthurian Theme,* edited by Tetsumaro Hayashi, Steinbeck Monograph Series no. 5 (Muncie, Indiana: The John Steinbeck Society of America, 1975), © 1975 by Tetsumaro Hayashi. Reprinted by permission of the author and the editor.

"Steinbeck's Strong Women: Feminine Identity in the Short Stories" by Marilyn L. Mitchell from *Southwest Review* 61, no. 3 (Summer 1976), © 1976 by Marilyn L. Mitchell. Reprinted by permission.

"John Steinbeck: Novelist as Scientist" by Jackson J. Benson from *Novel: A Forum on Fiction* 10, no. 3 (Spring 1977), © 1977 by Novel Corporation. Reprinted by permission.

"Steinbeck and Nature's Self: *The Grapes of Wrath*" by John J. Conder from *Naturalism in American Fiction: The Classic Phase* by John J. Conder, © 1984 by the University Press of Kentucky. Reprinted by permission of the publishers.

"Living for Writing" by Anthony Burgess from *But Do Blondes Prefer Gentle-*

men? Homage to Qwert Yuiop and Other Writings by Anthony Burgess, © 1986 by Liana Burgess. Reprinted by permission of McGraw-Hill Book Company.

"*Of Mice and Men:* The Dream of Commitment" by Louis Owens from *John Steinbeck's Re-Vision of America* by Louis Owens, © 1985 by the University of Georgia Press. Reprinted by permission.

"Abra: The Indestructible Woman in *East of Eden*" (originally entitled "Steinbeck") by Mimi Reisel Gladstein from *The Indestructible Woman in Faulkner, Hemingway, and Steinbeck* by Mimi Reisel Gladstein, © 1986 by Mimi Reisel Gladstein. Reprinted by permission of the author and UMI Research Press, Ann Arbor, Michigan.

Index

Modern Critical Views

Continued from front of book